Sculpting 101:

A Primer for the Self-taught Artist
Second Edition

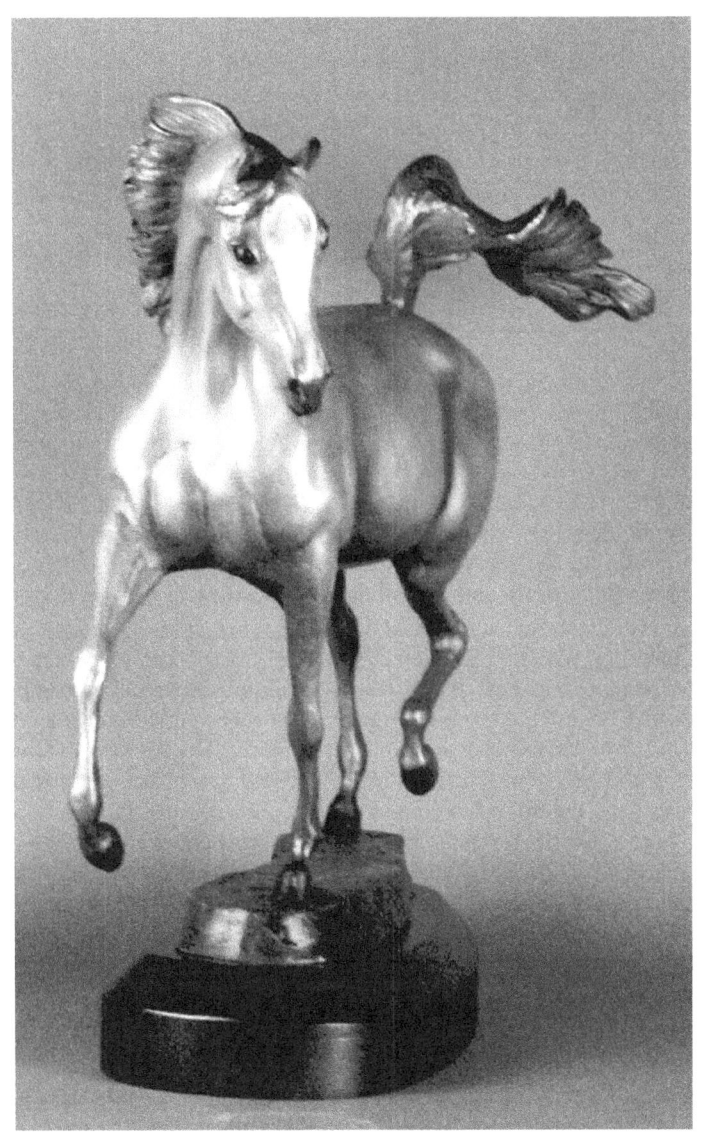

Lynda Sappington

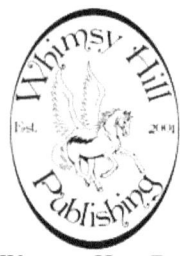

A WHIMSY HILL BOOK
Whimsy Hill Publishing
West Alexandria, Ohio, USA
WWW.WHIMSYHILL.COM
© 2008 Lynda Sappington

First Printing November 2008. Printed and bound in the United States of America. All Rights Reserved. No part of this book may be reproduced or transmitted in any form or by any means, electronic or mechanical, including photocopying, recording, or by an information storage or retrieval system—except by a reviewer, who may quote brief passages in a review to be printed in magazines or newspapers or on the web—without permission in writing from the publisher.

ISBN 10: 0-9723805-3-9 (Trade Paperback)
ISBN 13: 978-0-9723805-3-9 (Trade Paperback)

Notes on the Art:
Cover: "Friesian Elegance" Lynda Sappington © 2007, 22 1/2" L x 11 1/2" H x 9 1/2" W
Inside Cover: "Captivating" Lynda Sappington © 2006, 13" L x 11" H x 4 1/2" W
All Photos, Illustrations and Artwork © Lynda Sappington. All Rights Reserved.

Acknowledgements:
The author wishes to thank the artists who have given so generously of their time and expertise to help me learn the "how to" of sculpting and marketing my work: **Shary Akers**, an equine artist with exquisite talent, who invited this fledgling artist into her home to learn how to make molds, cast waxes and cast paper; **Marcia Van Woert**, a canine artist with limitless imagination, who has shared her marketing expertise and tips on painting, sculpting and jewelry, as well as sources for materials and services; **Elin Pendleton**, a fabulous painter who has shared her enthusiasm and marketing expertise with me quite generously; **Candi Farmer**, a graphic artist who nudged, pushed, pulled and pummeled me into getting back into art after years of my believing I had no artistic talent. Thanks also to **Dave Scott**, now retired from Scott Art Casting, and the folks at **Tallix Foundry**, for letting me take pictures of two kinds of bronze pours. Thanks to my daughter, **Jennifer Truett**, for helping me understand the finer points of dressage so I can accurately depict them. Thanks to **Diane Soper**, my basemaker, whose creative ideas for bases is a great help to me. Most of all, I need to thank my wonderful, creative and very patient husband, **John Sappington**, who takes days off work to put up and take down my booth at shows, fixes my computer or helps me with computing problems, and is a general all around good guy. I could not do this work without his support, and that's the absolute truth. The Christian fish symbol is carved into all of my sculptures to give praise to God for giving me this gift, as well as for loving me "warts and all." I did nothing to deserve the gifts He's given me, and I'm humbled and honored by His generosity.

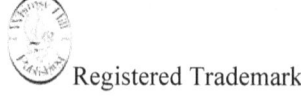 Registered Trademark

For information please contact:

Whimsy Hill Publishing, 15401 Eaton Pike, West Alexandria OH 45381-9610 USA
WWW.WHIMSYHILL.COM

Table of Contents

Chapter 1

Sculpture Materials

Sculptures can be created using wood, stone, paper, metal, glass, clay, plaster, concrete, all kinds of materials. Many sculpture materials, such as stone and glass, are "one of a kind" pieces, with the features of the material itself (the colors of the glass, the grain of the stone) being part of the design. You can make a mold of a sculpture in any of these materials and cast it in bronze, plaster, resin, paper, concrete, etc., if you want. However, most pieces intended for casting are originally created in clay of some kind.

Clays

There is a wide variety of clays on the market. I will explain the basics of how to use three of them: water-based clay; polymer clays like Sculpey® and Cernit®; and professional plastilene (also called "plasticene" or "plastilena").

Clays are wonderful to use because you can do both *subtractive* sculpting (where you remove material from the original sculpting medium as you would with stone or wood, for instance, until you get to the finished look you want) and *additive* sculpting (where you add to the original sculpting medium, as you do with clay, metal, or paper). If you make a mistake in clay, you can fix it easily because the medium is so forgiving. If you make a mistake in stone, you have to change your design to accommodate the changed area – or try to reattach the extra stone you removed and try to hide the mended spot (it can be done in some cases, but it's hard!)

Water-based Clay

Most school children start doing three-dimensional work with water-based clay, which is air dried, then fired in a kiln. This is the same general type of clay used by potters. There are many types of water-based clay (some of these clays are called "terra cotta," "raku," "sculpture clay" or "stoneware" clay depending on their consistency and numerous other variables). Essentially, this type of clay is clay soil harvested from the ground, then cleaned of rocks and debris, made a uniform texture and wetness (with water), then marketed in 25 lb. blocks in plastic bags. Potters who work on a wheel usually use very smooth *clay body* (type of clay) with no "grog" in it, sometimes called "throwing clay" (because they use it to throw pots on a wheel). Sculptors most often use "sculpting clay" which includes *grog* (pre-fired and pulverized clay) to give it more *body* (tensile strength). Some clays, such as raku, are too porous to be used as vessels for fluids and always have a coarse feel to them. Sculptures can be done quite well in raku clay, but those pieces will have a rougher surface texture than if they were done in sculpture clay. (However, because raku is so porous, it's also more forgiving about trapped air, which means less chance of it blowing up when it's fired. This attribute of raku makes it a good clay for beginners, in my opinion.) These different characteristics are things you need to consider when choosing your clay, if you choose to work in water-based clay.

Water-based clay must be kept moist by misting it lightly with water from a squirt bottle every so often while you're working on it. Then the finished sculpture needs to be hollowed out to no more than a one-inch thickness in any part of the finished sculpture for the piece to fire properly. The piece must be allowed to dry out slowly, with the piece wrapped in plastic at first so it doesn't dry too quickly. After the clay has dried a few days (depending on its size and thickness), the plastic can be loosened, then removed completely, as it dries out. Thin places (like the edges of tiles, or extended parts like arms on a figurative piece), need to be kept wrapped in plastic longer so they don't dry faster than the body of the piece. (If they dry faster than the rest of the piece, they may crack or fall off the piece.)

When the piece is completely dry, it is fired in a kiln (*bisque firing*) which is the only firing needed if the piece is sculpture and will be stained, painted or patinaed somehow. Bisque firing will harden the piece adequately for display, but if the piece is to be functional or displayed outdoors, it will need to be fired to near the point of *vitrification* (where it's almost liquid – the highest cone level marked for that kind of clay) to be as non-porous and hard as possible. If the piece will be glazed (like pottery or tiles), it will need a second firing (after the bisque firing) for the glazes to be fired.

The *cone* referred to above is the measurement of heat in a kiln. A cone made to melt at a certain temperature is installed in a cut-off switch in the kiln for each firing of the kiln. When the kiln reaches that temperature, the cone slumps, thus tripping the switch and turning off the kiln. Cones are rated at .06 (very low fire) to 10 (very high fire). It's safest to have an experienced person fire your pieces when you're first learning. Working with a kiln is a complicated business and can be dangerous if you aren't aware of all the safety precautions required.

Water-based clay is touchy and will blow up in the kiln if you trap air inside the piece. That's why I recommend beginners who are teaching themselves to sculpt to start with polymer clay like Sculpey or Super Sculpey – it's a more forgiving medium. There is a detailed discussion of water-based clay on **page 11.**

Polymer Clays

Sculpey®, Super Sculpey®, Sculpey III®, Cernit® and Fimo® are some of the best-known polymer clays currently on the market. They all bake in a kitchen oven to a hard finish. The finished products can be sanded, drilled, painted, stained, etc.

The processes of using the polymer clay products are simple and work basically the same for all the polymer clay products. I recommend regular (white) Sculpey for children because it's soft and easy to work with, as well as being non-toxic. It also has a decently long shelf life and is fairly inexpensive. Super Sculpey (which is peach or "flesh" colored) is the professional grade material, used by doll-makers and sculptors because of its durable nature. Sculpey III, Cernit or Fimo, which come in numerous colors, can be used as they come from the package, or be kneaded together to make more colors. These colored polymer clays are used to make ornaments, milleflore beads or buttons, jewelry, all kinds of things. These Sculpey III-type products are too expensive, in my opinion, to use for serious sculpture, but they are fine and a lot of fun to use for small pieces like cartoon or holiday-type figurines (snowmen, teddy bears, etc.). The nice thing about using the colored clays for Christmas trees, Santa figurines, etc., is that no finishing is needed because the color is in the clay.

When you buy polymer clay, be sure to open the box and press on the clay – if it's soft and gives easily to pressure, it's fresh and will be good to work with. (If you're buying Sculpey III or one of the other clays that come in cellophane wrappers, just press on the wrapper, don't unwrap the clay.) If the clay is stiff and hard, it may be old, or it may have partially baked in the delivery truck (I know of cases where this has happened). Don't buy stiff, hard polymer clay, you'll just frustrate yourself. You can get a lot of information on using polymer clay on www.sculpey.com. There is more detailed information on using polymer clay on **page 14**.

Plastilene

Plastilene (also called "plasticine") is the clay used by most professional sculptors who will be producing castings in bronze. It's an oil-based clay that doesn't harden or dry out. I've used some plastilene in four or five pieces before I felt it was too dry to be useful anymore. I get my original sculpture and armature back from the foundry once the mold is made so I can reuse the materials as much as possible.

Unlike water-based clay and the polymer clay products, plastilene will never give you a "finished product" – a mold and casting must be made. Professional sculptors also work in wax, plaster, stone, wood, metal, water-based clay, polymer clays, epoxy resins, and anything else that does the job. For the purposes of this book, we will stick with plastilene, polymer clay products and water-based clay as an introduction to sculpting.

As a sculptor who produces sculptures mostly in bronze and cold-cast porcelain, I use plastilene nearly all the time. I prefer plastilene that is non-sticky, soft enough to get the flow I want in manes and tails (since I mostly do equine art), and firm enough to hold thin, tiny details like ears and eyelids. I often combine clays, using relatively soft clay for most of the body, and harder clay for ears and anything else that "sticks out," such as a hoof that isn't attached to the base. I may use very hard clay or wax for horseshoes so I can sculpt them off the horse and then attach them without the hoof or the shoe losing detail or shape.

No matter what color, hardness or brand of plastilene clays I use, I only use *non-sulphur clays*. Clays containing sulphur not only can react badly with mold rubber, but many people (particularly those with lung problems like asthma) have allergic reactions to the sulphur in the clay. If you do use sulphur-bearing clay, you or your foundry will probably have to coat your finished sculpture in shellac or varnish to make a seal between the sulphur and the rubber mold material. This barrier layer can soften fine detail, so just avoid the problem by using non-sulphur clay in the first place. Talk to your foundry about which clays work best with their mold material.

You need to do your own research to find out which clay suits your needs. There are a lot of companies producing plastilene. Most will send you small samples if you request them. Chavant is one such manufacturer. To receive a sample kit of Chavant clays, you can call 1-800-Chavant or visit their Website at www.chavant.com. Sculpture House and The Compleat Sculptor (see "Tools" below for contact info) both carry a variety of clays. The one I use most of the time is Classic Clay which I order from Arizona Sculpture (www.arizonasculpture.com). It's listed under "J.F. McCaughin Clay & Waxes." Classic and Chavant are the preferred clays of professionals, although many still use Roma Prima (available from Sculpture House and The Compleat Sculptor – see the "tools" section below for contact info).

Tools

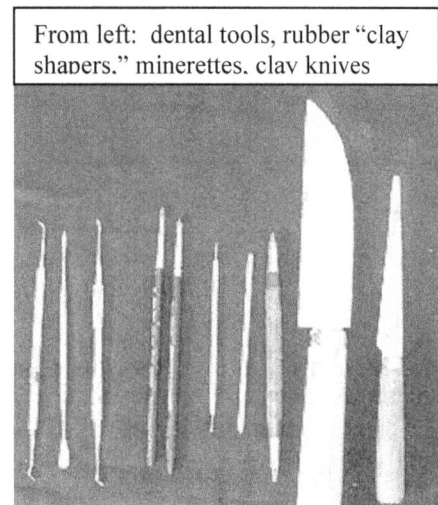
From left: dental tools, rubber "clay shapers," minerettes, clay knives

Tools can be anything – your fingers, plastic flatware, wooden rods, lengths of wire – but having an assortment of shapes in wooden or nylon tools is a good start. These can be purchased at many art or craft stores. If you can't find what you're looking for there, go to www.sculpt.com (or call 1-800-9-SCULPT) to see The Compleat Sculptor's line of tools, or check Sculpture House's line (see www.sculpturehouse.com for a list of their retailers near you). These are two of the biggest suppliers in the country. There are many others, as well.

Don't get overwhelmed by the variety of tools you see. Buy a couple of things at a time, find out what feels best in your hand, then buy accordingly. I prefer stainless steel dental tools, large to tiny (actual dental tools, usually spoon shaped or a small rounded blade bent at a 90° angle), and certain *ribbon* (with a loop of rounded or flattened wire at each end in a variety of shapes) tools. These are good for smoothing and removing clay quickly. The spoons are good for detail work (The first two tools in each of these pictures are the ones I use the most).

You can find sets of dental tools for sale on auction sites like www.ebay.com from time to time, or at flea markets. Many of the tools in these sets are useless for sculpting in plastilene because they're small sharp-edged wires bent in various shapes for cleaning teeth. These may be great for cleaning teeth, but I find them of little use for the kind of sculpting I do. The dental tools that work best for me are the ones the dentist uses to create and shape fillings – he's sculpting when he's doing your fillings, and the tools he uses are great for sculptors too. Sometimes your dentist may give you old tools that aren't worth sharpening anymore. I've gotten several from my dentist, and he's even ordered special tools for me I couldn't find elsewhere. Make a friend of your dentist – it may help your sculpture!

Chapter 2

Armatures

If you sculpt a standing or running horse or a bust of a human head with no *armature* (a support for clay), the weight of the horse's body will collapse his legs, or the weight of the head will collapse the neck on the bust in no time. Learning to make a good armature isn't that hard, but you need some guidelines to help you get started. There are many ways to make armatures. I'll go over some of the ones that I've found to be the most useful.

An armature requires a very strong central core firmly attached to the *working surface* (the board that's the working base for the sculpture). The materials and shape you use are determined by what you're sculpting.

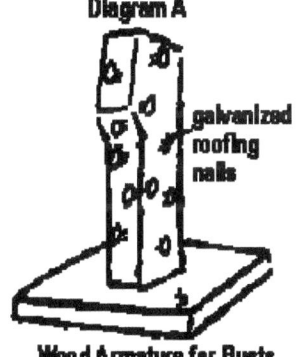

Diagram A

galvanized roofing nails

Wood Armature for Busts

The following armature designs are for tabletop-sized sculptures. Life-size or monumental-size sculptures require a steel rebar armature that probably should be made by your foundry or a more experienced sculptor the first few times you work that size. There will be more on life-sized work on **page 50.**

First determine the size and shape of your finished sculpture. Then prepare a board (the "working surface" mentioned above, which is not the base for your finished sculpture) that will be large enough to give you plenty of open space beyond the largest dimensions of the sculpture. It's easier for the foundry to build the mold around the piece if you use a generous board as your working surface. I use plywood as my working surface most of the time. (Never EVER use particle board, chipboard, beadboard or paneling – they aren't strong enough to support the armature if you have to ship the piece to the foundry!) It's also a good idea to shellac the working surface so the clay will clean off of it easily (or you can use a painted board or one of those shelves that's coated in Formica®).

If you're doing a piece that will have a broad base, such as a bust, you can use a piece of wood for the armature, such as the 2" x 2" shown in Diagram A above. (The extra piece on the front near the top is another 2x2 attached to take up space in the face of the bust.) Use two or three screws, never just one (or it will turn around as you work) to attach the wooden armature to the working surface so it stands vertically. Then hammer in short nails with broad heads (like large carpet tacks or roofing nails) all around the wood. The nails give the clay something to hang on to, so it won't move around. You can also wrap a lightweight aluminum armature wire from nail to nail to give even more gripping surface, but it isn't always necessary. Experience will tell you when you need to wrap wire around your nails. This type of armature is commonly used with water-based clay, but can also be used with plastilene.

Steel and plastilene clay have a bad chemical reaction to each other (the clay turns black and crumbly after prolonged exposure to bare steel), so be sure to spray any nonaluminum metal with polyurethane or paint it with varnish or shellac before applying your clay.

Pretty much anything can be an armature if you can make it stay where you want it. I've used foam board house insulation with nails stuck in it for an armature. The tricky part was getting it to stick to the working surface and not move. I've also used metal mesh, aluminum foil, spray foam insulation and other things. Use what works best for the material and situation, and what you have on hand or can obtain easily. And remember, if you have to ship it, you'll have to build it a lot stronger than if you're hand-carrying it to the foundry

Traditional armature wire and plumbing pipe armatures are the most versatile, and are used with plastilene. To make one of these for a tabletop-sized sculpture, you'll need 1/8" or 3/8" plumbing (1/8" for a smaller piece, larger pipe for larger pieces): a floor flange, straight pipe and connectors to make it the height you want, and a plumbing "T" pipe. You can use either galvanized or PVC pipe. I use galvanized most of the time, so I can twist the plumbing T to a different angle if I want to, which is harder to do with PVC, especially if you glue the PVC in place.

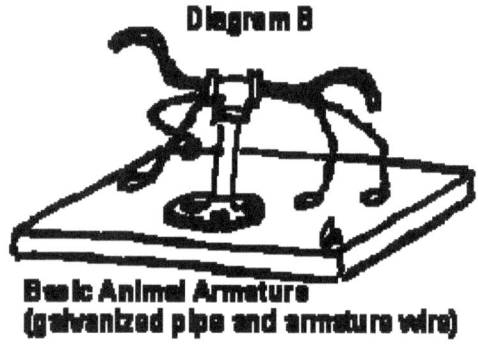

Diagram B

Basic Animal Armature (galvanized pipe and armature wire)

First you have to decide if the armature support is going into the bottom of your piece or into the side. If you're sculpting a standing or running animal, having the pipe go from the bottom is easiest. If the animal is rearing or leaping, or you have a lot of detail directly beneath it (such as a jump) then you may want to have the support be off to one side (see "Back Iron Armatures" on **page 8**). The T needs to be centered in the thickest part of the animal so you won't hit it while sculpting. Assemble your pipes as shown in Diagram B.

Now comes the "fun" (creative, non-plumbing) part: the wires. You have to determine the size and shape of your finished piece, then put wires of the proper strength in place to hold the clay. They have to be strong enough to hold the clay up and not sag. Make the armature strong enough to start with and you'll have far fewer headaches (yes, this is the voice of experience talking!).

After you determine the size of the finished piece, measure off more aluminum wire than you think you'll need for the armature. Use heavy wire for the main armature sections. For a four-legged animal like a horse, cat or lion, one heavy wire forms the head, neck, back and tail. Lighter wires form each pair of legs (front and back) or small wire doubled and twisted can form individual legs. More details on building the armature are in the "Back Iron Armature" section on **page 8**.

Armature wire is available at sculpture supply houses (Arizona Sculpture, Sculpture House, The Compleat Sculptor, through catalogs, etc.) **Do NOT use steel wire unless you coat it with polyurethane or**

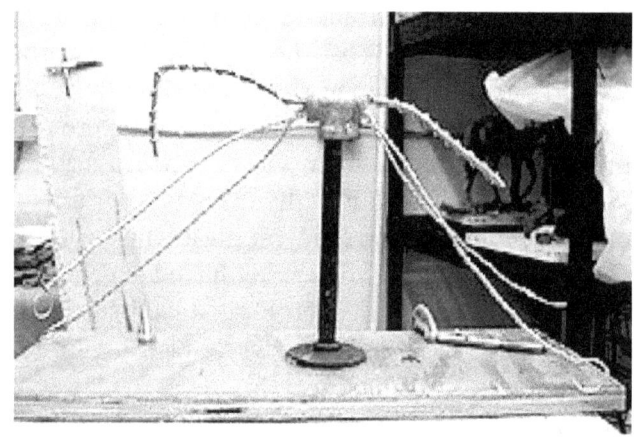

shellac. Electric fence wire will suffice, but it isn't made to be as flexible as real armature wire, nor does it come in the variety of sizes armature wire does. You can reuse the armature wire if you want to and are patient enough to straighten it again, so invest in the right tools to start with.

Once you have your main wire (the heaviest wire, which goes from head to tail in the horse) measured, cut a piece of the thin aluminum wire and wrap the length of the big wire. Wrap all of the straight wires you use in the same way. (Twisted wires don't need wrapping.) Wrapping the wire gives the clay something to bite into, so it doesn't slide or twist around. Fold your thin wires (for the legs) in half and put a pencil or nail in the loop formed by folding it. Hold the free ends with pliers and turn the pencil or nail around until you have the wires twisted tightly together. For a leg that will be held up, the wires will need to be twisted very tightly. Legs that touch the base don't need their wires twisted as tightly.

Insert the prepared wires into the T and get them placed appropriately. Hold them in place (at the T) and push toothpicks in the T from each end to make them stay put. Break off the excess of each toothpick inserted into the T. Continue to insert toothpicks until you can't get any more in either opening of the T. If you prefer hardware to toothpicks, get two small plumbing screw clamps and put one over the wires on each end of the T. Push them against the T and screw them tight. Be sure the tail of the screw clamps' ends will be deep inside your sculpture, not close to the surface.

Your animal's legs (or whatever parts are sticking out) will probably have a loop at the end from the wire being doubled over and twisted (see photo above). If the leg is the desired length, you can insert a screw into this loop and screw it to the board. If the wires are longer than the leg needs to be, you can create grass (or a floor, whatever) out of clay, then stick the loops into that. This second method is a good one when you aren't positive where you want the legs positioned. Just be sure the loops are large enough that they will hold a lot of clay when you stick them into (or under) the clay base so they won't move. Another way is to staple the loops to the board, then build the clay over the loops, which is what I do most of the time.

If you're working with **water-based clay**, you will have to remove the armature and hollow the piece out, then reassemble the sculpture and let it dry out completely before you can fire it. Details start on **page 11**. You will have a finished piece you can stain or glaze after the piece is fired. A mold can be made of the finished piece if you want to make an *edition* (copies of the original, usually signed, numbered and limited to a specific number). (NOTE: Wire armatures are hard to use with water-based clay. Wooden armatures are much easier to use with water-based clay.)

If you're working with a **polymer clay**, internal armatures can be left in place forever, but you'll need a different support system. More information on working with polymer clay is on **page 14**. Molds can be made from a baked polymer clay piece if you want to make an edition from your original. "Dragon's Dilemma" (at right) was originally a Super Sculpey piece. I had a mold made and cast it as an edition.

If you're working with **plastilene**, you will need to have a mold made of your sculpture before you have a finished piece, but you won't need to set it aside to dry or to remove it from its armature. See **page 27** for more information on mold-making and casting. Once the mold is made, doing an edition is easy. See **page 47** for more information on editions.

Back-Iron Armatures

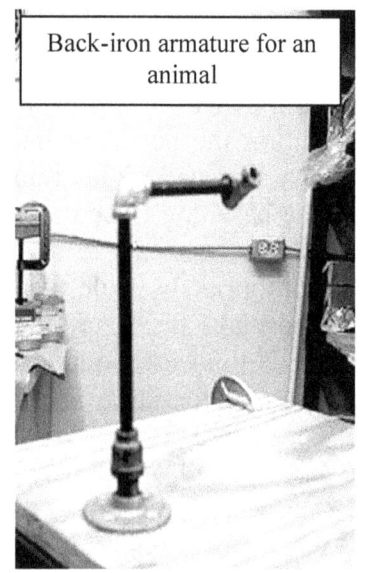

Back-iron armature for an animal

I made this armature for "Skydancer," a jumping horse suspended above clouds by a thin line of bronze that is *patinaed* (colored by various acids and other media being applied to the bronze) a light blue to represent the sky.

The armature shown here uses fairly small (1/4") pipe with a connector to a larger pipe because I couldn't find a floor flange that small. For a back-iron armature, you will need a floor flange, pipe of whatever length you need for height, a 45° or a 90° elbow joint (depending on how you want the pipe to go into the piece – I've used a 90° angle elbow joint here), another length of pipe to go between the elbow and the sculpture, and the T joint.

This style of armature, where the support pipe is not directly under the sculpture, is often called a "back iron" armature because in *figurative* (human) sculpture, the support pipe goes into the middle of the person's back, as shown on the "in progress" piece at right. Most of my pieces are made with the pipe coming in underneath, into the center of the body mass of the horse. For the jumping horse, where the under-belly and base detail (the clouds in "Skydancer's" base) are really important, the side-mounted armature seemed the best choice. Foundry workers have no problem repairing the hole in the side or the belly of the horse. Whenever you see a leaping animal sculpture, it was probably done with a back- or side-iron armature like this one.

The wooden working surface is shellacked so the plastilene clay will not stick to it, and so there won't be any splinters to get in the clay (or the sculptor's hands!). Remember, when steel or galvanized pipes are used, they need to be sprayed with polyurethane to coat it, or painted with shellac, so there won't be a chemical reaction between the steel and the plastilene. As long as the pipe is sealed, there should be no problems

I begin by cutting aluminum armature wire longer than it needs to be. The heavy wire will support the horse's head, neck, body and tail, with smaller wire wrapped around it to give the clay something to "bite." Smaller wires are doubled and twisted to form each leg, or each pair of legs, whatever works best for the piece. The tighter the wires are twisted, the stronger they are and the more clay they'll support, so for tightly folded legs, or legs extended out (not hanging down as if the horse is standing), the wire has to be tightly twisted to support the clay's weight.

Aluminum wire is used because it's both strong enough to hold the clay and soft enough to manipulate easily, plus it doesn't have any chemical reaction with clay. Steel coat hanger wire, for instance, would have a chemical reaction with plastilene clay, and is brittle and inflexible (for fine or curved movement), so it isn't the best choice for armature wire.

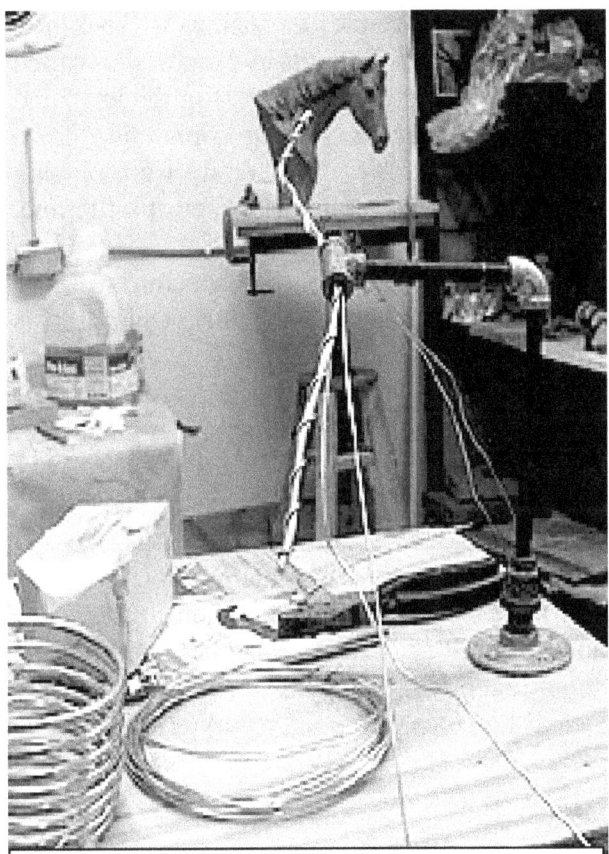

Armature wires in place. Leg wires not cut to length yet, and wires are not "shaped" to their final form.

Look at all the wires that pass through this T-joint. In order to stabilize the wires, I will shove in toothpicks and break them off where they stick out past the end of the T. I continue to shove toothpicks in from each end until I can't get any more in. I make sure to break off the toothpick as close to the T as possible so I don't stick my fingers when I'm working. The wires all have to be held in place as the toothpicks are put in place so they are in the right position once they're stabilized.

Some sculptors use *pipe clamps*, those little metal strips with a screw in them that get smaller as you screw it in. I don't like these clamps for pieces as small as most of mine, because I usually wind up hitting the clamp while sculpting at some point. Toothpicks are less trouble for me to work with. You have to decide which method is most comfortable to you.

On the completed armature, I normally make the legs way too long so I can sculpt to the length of leg I want and cut off the excess. Some artists will make the armature exactly the right size to start with. I tend to let the sculpture tell me where it wants to go for these tabletop sized pieces, so I like an armature that moves and adjusts easily. The same type of armature is used for modeling people, with the T joint set upright and the wires arranged differently (no tail, for instance! ☺)

The "brick" on the sculpture stand above is a new wrapped two pound block of Roma Prima plastilene clay, which I don't use anymore, but is a good clay to start with (partly because you can buy it in small bricks, while the Classic Clay I use now is purchased in 10-12 lb. slabs, usually in 50 pound case lots). The large horse bust in the background is "Destiny" just before he went to the foundry to be cast in bronze. He was sculpted in Chavant Le Beau Touché, a non-sulfur plastilene that has a feel similar to water clay. It's too soft a clay for smaller pieces, but for a piece this size, it was quite nice. It has an odor that bothers my asthma, so if you have sensitive lungs, buy a small amount to see how you react to its fumes before investing in a large quantity. Due to my sensitivity to this odor, I've stopped using Chavant clays. Their non-sulfur clays go through the same presses as the sulfur-bearing ones, so the clay must pick up the sulfur smell there. Other than the smell, it's great clay. You have to try a lot of clays and choose which one pleases you most. For me, it's Classic Clay. For you, it could be one of the many other brands.

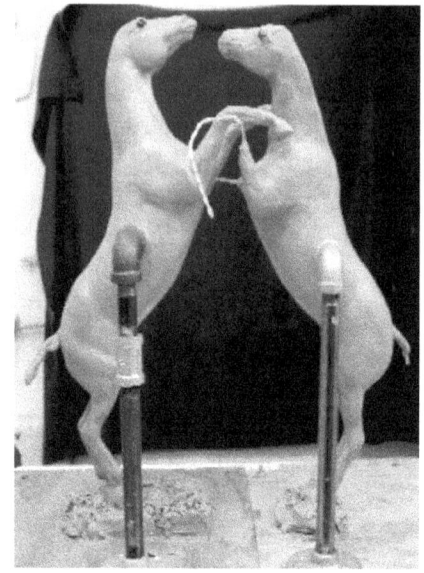

As another example of using a back-iron armature, here's a work-in-progress called "Horseplay," showing my horse, Jack (on the left), and my husband's horse, Pepper, rearing as high as a horse can go without falling over. They really were playing here, and the photo I took of it was a shot of a lifetime, capturing them at the peak of the action. Here I've used two back-iron armatures on two separate working surfaces made to be attached together when I was ready to "join" the horses.

Look at the working surface and notice the screws between the two horses. The horse on the right, Pepper, was built on a double thickness of wood with the top edge extending out an inch or so, which covers the lower layer of Jack's base which extends out a matching inch. The two bases thus interlock, and by having the nuts on the top of the working surface, I can easily detach them if I need to work on the horses' bellies again, for instance. I built each horse separately and got his body as detailed as I could before putting them together. The grass under their feet may be done as separate "puddles" of grass so each horse can be sold separately as well as together – I'm still deciding about that.

Chapter 3
At last! We start sculpting!

Sculpting with water-based clay

Water-based clay is just that, clay-type dirt mixed with water (and yes, some folks still "do it themselves" with clay from their yard – but commercially available clay is evenly mixed and has no rocks or impurities in it, so to me, the time saved is worth the cost).

You can use an armature for working with water clay. For a life-sized bust, for instance, have a 2" x 2" board mounted vertically to the working surface, add shorter 2 x 2 to the front at the top (nail or screw it in) -- this will be where the face goes. Tap roofing nails in all over the boards so the clay will have something to grip. (This armature design is shown in Diagram A on **page 5**.)

Prior to putting your clay on your armature, you may need to "wedge" it. To do this, use your *cut-off wire* (a tool that is a wire with two handles) and cut a section off your block of clay. Then pound the chunk of clay by throwing it on a sturdy, plastic-covered table. Throw it hard! This is one of the most fun things about using water clay! It's a great way to vent your frustrations! Wedging gets any trapped air out of the clay, a must to prevent your work exploding in the kiln. (Some water clay comes already wedged and ready to use – ask your dealer if the clay you're buying needs to be wedged or not. And remember, any clay you return to the bag will need to be wedged again before you can use it.) Be sure as you wedge, when you fold over the clay to compress the pile, press it in HARD so you don't trap any air, then throw it hard on the table to beat any remaining air out of the clay.

To add clay as you sculpt, always press it in very firmly, making sure you aren't trapping any air. Air pockets don't have to be very large to cause serious damage, and when your piece blows up in the kiln, the exploding pieces fly around and damage the other things in the kiln too – not a good way to ensure friendships with the others who are sharing your kiln-time! Add clay a little at a time, no big slabs or chunks. Sculpting in clay is both an adding and a subtracting process: you can put on too much clay to start with and carve away what isn't your subject, or you can just put on the amount you need, if you prefer to work that way.

Always clean your tools and working area used with water-based clay when the clay is still wet, and clean with a wet paper towel. Do NOT sweep up dried clay – wet it and wipe it up. The clay dust is hazardous to your lungs and can cause silicosis, a very serious lung disease.

As you work on your sculpture, you'll need to use a spray bottle filled with water to re-moisten it from time to time. You don't want it "slimy" but you also can't allow it to dry out unevenly. The thinnest parts (nostrils, legs, fingers, horse's ears, etc.) will dry out the most quickly, so pay special attention to them. But if you over-wet them, parts of them can fall off, so don't be TOO generous with your water!

It's easier with water clay to use a wooden armature rather than a wire armature, because you will have to cut that sculpture off of the armature. If it's entwined with wire, you're going to have a serious lesson in patience while trying to get it off the armature without damaging the work too much!

As with any sculpture, try to avoid deep *undercuts* (places in the sculpture where the mold will catch and stick instead of pulling off smoothly). You can check for undercuts by inserting the tip of a tool behind a part that is raised up or sticks out. If the tip of the tool can't be seen, you have an undercut that needs to be filled in enough to make the mold pull off cleanly. If you should decide at some point you want to have more than one copy of this sculpture, the mold and castings will all be easier to deal with if there aren't serious undercuts. (How deep an undercut you can use is determined by the mold material used to copy your piece – rubber molds are relatively forgiving of undercuts and tight places; plaster molds aren't forgiving at all.)

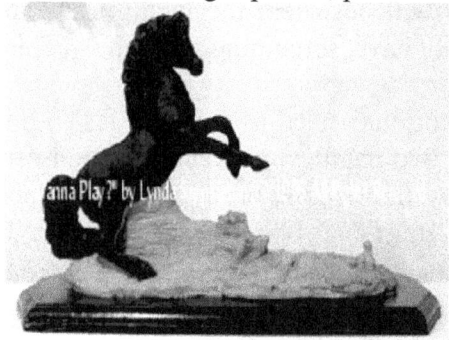

"Wanna Play?" shown at left, is a piece I did in water clay when I was first learning to sculpt. It didn't require an armature because of the way it was made. Projecting things, like the legs on this pony, need clay support rods to keep them from sagging as they dry. As the piece dries out (after you've finished sculpting it), you can usually remove these supports. If you fire the piece with these unfired clay supports in place, they will become part of your finished sculpture whether you like it or not, so remember to remove them! (Notice the rock under the pony supporting his belly. Without that rock, he would not have stood on his legs, since he had no armature.)

When you finish each day's work on the sculpture, keep the piece damp by laying a wrung-out tea towel over the top or over the thickest parts, and wrapping the whole thing, sculpture and towel, tightly in plastic. This wrapping is a good use for dry cleaner's bags. Due to their softness, it's easy to wrap the piece tightly (squeezing out the air) and yet not put pressure on delicate parts.

Before you cut your piece apart, make a *nest* for each section of your piece by twisting newspapers into a long tube, then form the twist of paper into a circle, with a depression in the center. Cover the newspaper with dry cleaner's plastic. (See picture on the next page).

After finishing the sculpting of the piece, watch for when the clay becomes <u>firm</u> but ***not leather-hard*** (leather-hard clay is not flexible and retains the impression of your fingernail if you press it into the surface – the clay's surface looks like a thick piece of leather at this point). Before the clay gets leather-hard (which can take a few hours to a few days), you will need to cut your sculpture in half (or more pieces, depending on the design) and remove the armature. Use your clay knife to cut where you will disturb the least detail – in a bust, for instance, you cut from the top of the head down each side in front of, or behind, the ears, depending on whether there's less detail in front or behind. Cut all the way to the armature (this is where you'll be glad you used wood!) and use your knife to slide the pieces apart and off the armature.

Once they're off the armature, lay each part in a prepared nest, then start hollowing the piece out. Make sure it's no thicker than 1" anywhere so it will fire properly.

To check your thickness, insert a needle from the inside where you've been hollowing it out, to the outside of the piece. Place your finger in line with the needle and slowly push the needle through until you feel it just reach the outside of the piece. (See picture below.) Put your thumbnail on the needle at the spot where it meets the clay on the inside, withdraw it from the clay and see how much of the needle was inside (remember, you want the clay to be no more than an inch thick). The resulting pin hole inside the sculpture will actually be good for it, letting gases escape during firing, so don't worry about refilling it, just rub your finger over the spot on the surface of the sculpture to make sure there is no damage there.

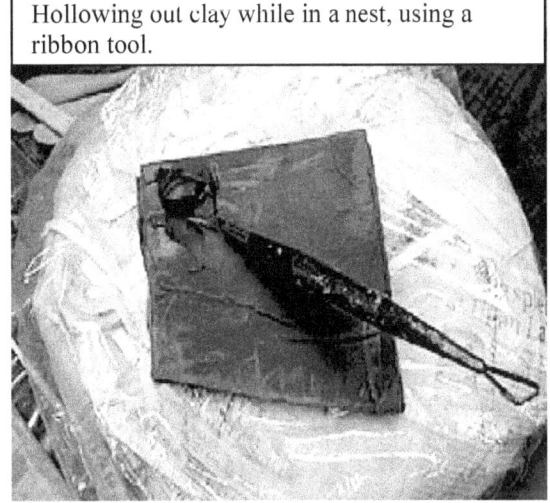

Hollowing out clay while in a nest, using a ribbon tool.

If your sculpture was made without an armature and isn't large enough to need to be cut in half, you can cut it off the working base (using the cut-off wire is best), and lay it in a nest. Then hollow it out from underneath to be no more than 1" thick.

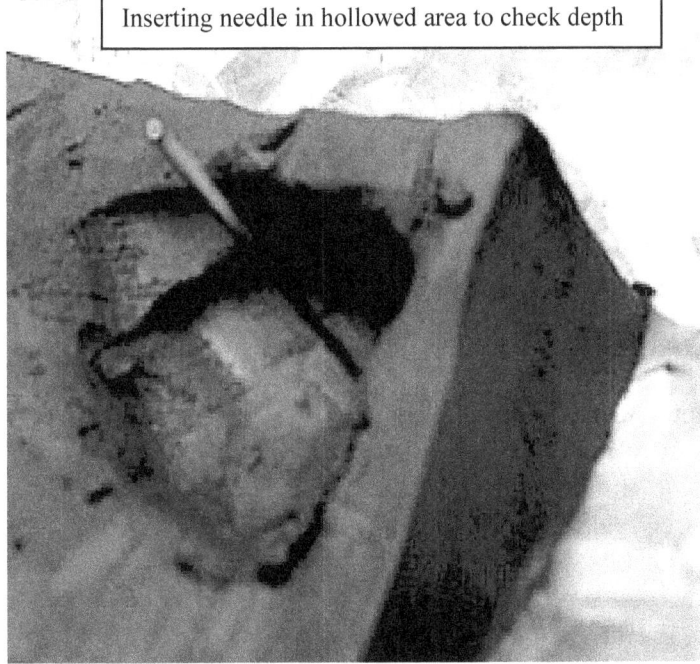

Inserting needle in hollowed area to check depth

When the piece is hollowed out to the proper thickness, *crosshatch* (score the surface in two different directions, making a pattern of intersecting lines) the edges. Apply *slip* (water mixed with a little bit of clay to create a consistency like Elmer's glue) to all cut and crosshatched edges, and re- assemble the sculpture care- fully so no air is trapped in the seam. (It's wise to have someone help you at this point – you'll be grateful for that extra pair of hands while you're reassembling the sculpture.) Replace/repair any detail that was marred and settle your piece in a nest. (If the piece will stand by itself, such as a small reclining animal, set it on a shelf or a piece of drywall to dry and don't worry about the nest).

The drying process can take days (for a thin tile) to weeks for a sculpture. Don't try to hurry it or you'll weaken the clay. Your finished sculpture must be allowed to dry slowly, as described above. Trapped water, like trapped air, will make it explode in the kiln, so it must get completely dry. Drying too quickly or unevenly can make the clay warp, slump or crack, so do your best to keep it drying evenly.

After the sculpture is completely finished, loosen the plastic wrap and let the piece dry out slowly -- dampen any thin parts LIGHTLY (just a couple of squirts with a spray bottle) every day or two, so they don't get too dry and brittle before the rest dries. Check the piece regularly; redampen the tea towel as needed (expect to breathe some mold when you open the wrapping!). You want the clay to dry out EVENLY, which can be tricky with some pieces.

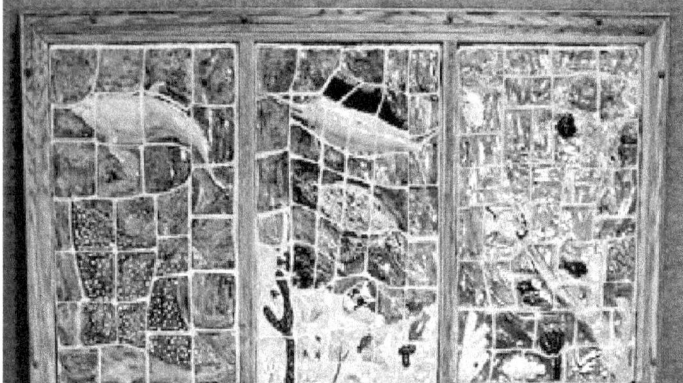

"Under the Sea," terra cotta mural, 3' x 6' in a custom made oak frame. These are the tiles shown in previous illustrations.

When your piece is leather-hard (which is soon after it starts drying), you can *burnish* (smooth) the surface by using the back of a spoon in small circles all over the piece to give it a more refined surface. After the sculpture is completely dry, you can fire it, then paint, stain or glaze it (which requires a second firing) and you have a finished piece. You can also sand a leather-hard piece very carefully, but wear a dust-protective mask if you do so. Breathing clay dust can cause silicosis in the lungs.

For more detailed instructions on working with water-based clay, find an art center or a ceramics or pottery store near you and ask the staff about lessons or a good book. These directions are VERY general. Water-based clay is tricky to work with. If this is the medium you want to use, please find a teacher or a good book on that specific subject!

Sculpting with Polymer Clay

Polymer clays can be sculpted with little or no armature, depending on what you're making. If you're making something that has no thin supports (like legs), then all you need to do is wad up some aluminum foil to be the "bulk" (thickest part) of your sculpture. You don't want to make polymer clay pieces thick – they work best if they're less than one inch thick. Also, this material is more expensive than the others mentioned, so it's smart to be conservative in using it.

Wad up your foil into a firm ball about ½" smaller than the bulk of whatever you're making.

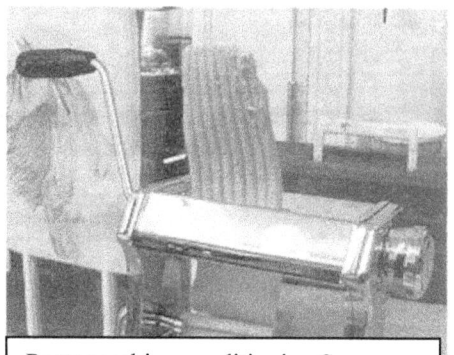

Pasta machine conditioning Super Sculpey.

Put your foil on a working surface covered with foil, which will make it easier for you to remove the original from the working surface and put it on oven-tolerant glass (like a glass casserole dish) for baking.

Using your fingers or a pasta machine (which is used only for this purpose and not for food preparation, shown in use on the previous page), knead the clay until it's soft and pliable. If the clay is still hard, try some Sculpey Diluent or vegetable oil worked into the clay. That will usually make it more workable. If the clay comes out of the box feeling too "wet," use a rolling pin and roll the whole brick of clay down to two inches thick. Then put that slab of clay between two pieces of copier paper, lay a heavy book on top, and in a few days the excess oils will have leached out. Lay the clay on your foil armature and work it into the surface of the foil. Keep applying clay until you have the piece in the size and basic shape you want.

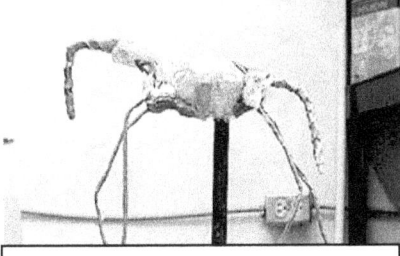

Armature wrapped in duct tape and bulked up with foil and metal mesh

If you want to do a polymer clay piece that's standing on legs, you will need stronger support. Thick legs are a good idea for this kind of project (like a Santa Claus in his boots – those thick legs are good support). For a four-legged animal with thin legs, get a wooden dowel rod and cut it to the length you will need to support the animal's stomach. Make an armature out of thin wire (or floral wire) and **cover the armature tightly with duct tape**. Polymer clay won't stick even to twisted wire very well, but it will stick to duct tape. Wrap foil or metal mesh around the bulky parts of the body (barrel, neck and rump of the horse, for instance), then start laying on clay as above. Insert your dowel rod under the animal's belly when you get it built up to the point of needing the rod to keep the piece from sagging or bending the legs. Once the piece is baked, you can remove the dowel rod and fill the dent in the horse's stomach with more Sculpey and re-bake, or fill the hole with vinyl spackle.

You can attach things like arms on a Santa, ears on a horse, etc., by sticking a straight piece of small gauge wire in the lump of clay that will be the arm or ear, then shove that into the sculpture, then blend the pieces together. The wire will help bear the weight of the appendage so it won't pull away from the body. In this instance, the wire doesn't have to be wrapped in duct tape to work.

Sculpey recommends you build your piece up ¼" thickness at a time, and bake it as you add each ¼" of thickness. This method is fine if you are completely certain where all the parts go before you start, because you can't change your mind partway through the piece if it's already had the initial layers baked. Since I work in plastilene more than Sculpey, I'm used to adding on clay, carving some off, changing my mind about a leg position, adjusting the armature, turning the head differently, etc., which makes using Sculpey's "bake as you go" procedure difficult for me. I'll show you how I do it below. But if you can do it Sculpey's way, you will have a better chance at good results.

One problem with polymer clay is that it can have a "memory" and it may "rebound" – in other words, if you sculpt sharp detail (like eyelids, for instance), then leave the piece overnight, the detail may soften during that time. If the piece started leaning one way at some point, it may always try to lean that way ("memory"). This is more of a problem with clay that started out stiff than with a really fresh batch, but you just need to be prepared for the clay to act this way. There are ways around these problems, but you may have to be creative with your solutions. When in doubt, call or email Sculpey's techies – they really know what they're doing. If you're using another brand of polymer clay, I'm sure they have technical assistants available as well.

Once you have your piece completely sculpted, you can support anything that needs it with a polymer clay column. "Good Morning" (right) needed a support under the mare and foal's chins, as well as one under the mare's belly. A wooden dowel rod will keep the piece upright while sculpting, and the piece can be baked with that dowel rod in place. You can also make polymer supports which will not stick to your sculpture as long as you don't press or work together the clay of the support with the clay of 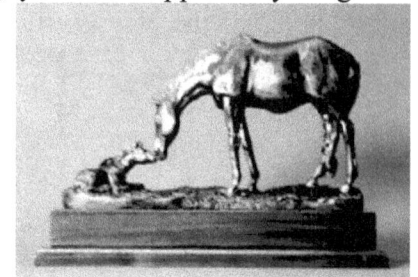 the sculpture. For this piece, which is made in Super Sculpey and has a wire armature but no exterior support (no back iron), I made supports of Super Sculpey. I made one for under the mare's belly, and one under her and the foal's chins.

To sculpt a free-standing horse in Super Sculpey with no grass under its feet (therefore, no base – the grass is what the base is either screwed or glued to), you'll need to make a full armature that will stand on its own legs. You can experiment with these by making miniatures the size of small Christmas ornaments. Use fine floral wire, two pieces twisted together so the clay will grip the clay well, and build an armature just like a regular one, but with no pipes. About midway along the length of wire that forms the horse's barrel, attach a long wire that goes up away from the horse's back. As you add foil, wire mesh, etc., to build up the armature, make certain this wire is still sticking straight out of the horse's back. Once you start putting clay on, make certain the horse will stand squarely on his feet by sitting him on a table or on a work surface every so often. Again, be certain the straight wire still comes up through his back.

Once the piece is finished, you will use the straight wire to hang the ornament from the wire oven rack set on the top setting in your oven. Bake him that way and he should turn out nice and solid and able to stand in his own feet. He'll also have a handy hanging wire at the top if you decide that this piece will be an ornament. If it won't be used as an ornament, just snip off the hanging wire at the surface.

Not all of your pieces will turn out well. Be patient with yourself and your art – you're learning an entirely new skill here. With these fragile little armatures, you need to be especially patient and not get upset if they don't all work properly.

There are three good methods to smooth your polymer clay and remove crumbs. The one I use most involves mixing Sculpey Diluent and Isopropol Alcohol 50/50, then applying this mixture with a small paintbrush. Another method is to use vegetable oil instead of the Diluent/alcohol mixture. I prefer a short bristled brush, such as an old oil painting filbert brush, or any small brush cut to have short stiff bristles (I cut one brush down to an angled point, similar to a deer-hoof shaped brush. The point gets into small detail without messing it up). Don't soak the piece, but use the brush to get down into the crevices and other places that are rough or otherwise not exactly the way you want them. The third method involves rubbing the piece with talcum powder and your fingers, but this only works on the places with not much detail, in my experience.

Baking the Super Sculpey Sculpture

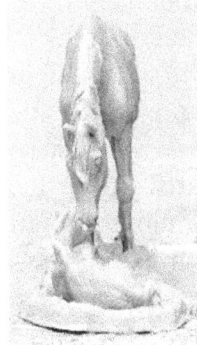

If your sculpture was created with a piece of foil laid on top of your working surface (as shown in the photo of "Good Morning" in the original Super Sculpey here), it should slide right off the working surface and onto the baking surface. If the foil tore and the clay is sticking to the working surface, slide a knife under there gently to free it. If you built it on a pipe armature, as I did for "Come On, Boys," (shown below), then you will have to bake it on the wooden working surface (which is not a problem, don't worry!)

These directions come directly from my Super Sculpey supplier and are applicable to <u>any small sculpture that does NOT have a pipe armature</u>:

"Use an oven thermometer to check your oven temperature. Put your sculpture on baking parchment, copy paper or index cards, in the bottom of a glass baking dish. Put the dish in the center of the oven, away from heating elements. Do not bake the clay at higher temperatures than recommended, and do not microwave it."

They also recommend you not put unbaked clay on fine furniture.

Look at the box the polymer clay came in to see how long and at what temperature to bake your sculpture. Super Sculpey is supposed to be baked **at 275° F/130° C for 15 minutes for every ¼" thickness.**

"Good Morning" (the mare and foal piece above), which was bulked up with foil and aluminum mesh, took over 40 minutes to bake. When they bake, you need to run your vent fan, because the fumes are smelly.

"Good Morning" was small enough to bake upright on a glass dish as

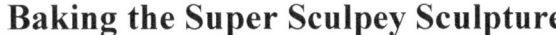

Laid on Polyfil, this piece has already baked 15 minutes. I have wrapped his hand to protect it from further baking.

recommended. "Come On, Boys" is 11" tall and too tall to bake in my oven. There are two ways to deal with this problem, but you MUST have a very strong armature in your piece to bake it this way. Plan ahead – if your piece will be too tall for your oven, make sure it won't be too long/wide for your oven, and that the armature is sturdy.

To bake an oversized piece like "Come On, Boys," you can build up pillows of Super Sculpey to lay your sculpture on. Or, you can do as I did, using pillows of Polyfil (you can buy bags of it for under $2 at craft or sewing stores – this baking took very little, maybe two handfuls). I laid a piece of plywood on my oven rack to keep the Polyfil in

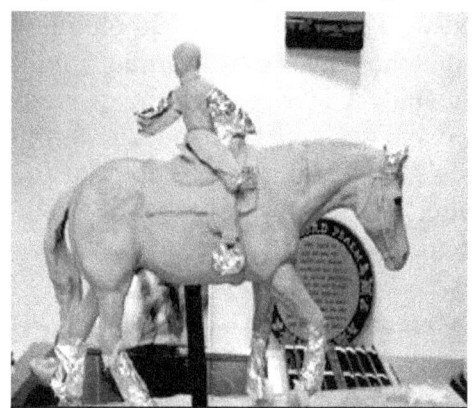

After 30 minutes of baking, wrapping parts in order from thinnest to thickest for each baking.

place, then piled up as much Polyfil as I thought I'd need. I carefully laid the sculpture on its side with the child's head toward my oven window so I could keep an eye on the thin parts. After the piece was lying down, I stuffed more Polyfil where it was needed and slid the rack into the pre-heated oven. (Note: There were no adverse fumes from the wood or the Polyfil. The Polyfil didn't even get hot to the touch.)

The following is very important if your sculpture has widely varying thicknesses like nearly any horse sculpture does. In the case of "Come On, Boys," the horse's body was built up with foil and metal mesh, but it's still quite thick compared to the thin parts like the horse's legs, the child's thumb, etc. If your piece has thin spots like this, after the first period of baking time (15 minutes per ¼" thickness, remember), take the sculpture out of the oven and **wrap strips of wet paper towel around the thin part, then cover the strip with foil.** Make sure the thin parts are totally surrounded with paper towel and foil. This process prevents cracking as the baking continues.

"Come On, Boys" took over an hour to bake because the horse's body is just over 3" thick. I kept taking the piece out and wrapping thicker and thicker parts until only the horse's barrel was left unwrapped.

Don't over-bake your piece! Trust the timetable – there's no real way to check that the piece is done. If it starts getting brown, it's baked too long. It may turn out with what look like "finger cuts" on the

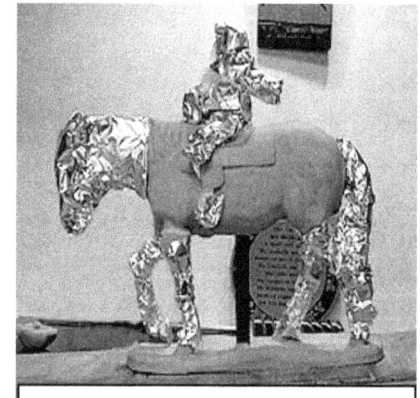

Wrapped for final baking period.

surface – small surface cracks in the clay – or even deep cracks. If this happens, the best way to repair it is to fill the cracks with a resin epoxy sculpting material that dries overnight, like Magic Sculpt (www.magicsculpt.com). I've found that it works best to apply the Magic Sculpt, then immediately wipe with a damp paper towel. By smoothing and removing the excess resin epoxy this way, I didn't have to sand the piece at all. Another way to repair cracks is to use vinyl spackle, followed by a damp paper towel to smooth it out and remove the excess.

To finish, sand your piece smooth if needed, then paint it with acrylic auto primer or painter's gesso and finish however you want, unless you're going to make a mold off of it. One nice way to finish this kind of piece is to paint it flat white (spray auto primer works well), then dip it in a can of wood stain (dark ones like walnut work best). Wipe the stain off the high spots, leaving it in the recesses, and it will look like antique ivory. Or you can paint the finished piece to look like a real horse if you want to.

If you're going to make a mold off your sculpture, don't paint or stain it, because paint and stain fill in detail. You want your mold to have the detail as sharp as what you sculpted in the piece.

If you want a finished piece with no mold-making or casting needed, or you need a piece to be hard so it can be shipped safely, polymer clays are a good way to go. And the fact that they're safe enough for kids to use makes them a great choice when you want to do family projects. Just be sure to wash your hands and work area well with soap and water when you're finished working.

Getting Started with Plastilene

To begin sculpting in plastilene, first I cover the armature with clay so there are no sharp pieces to catch me unaware, and to stabilize the armature in the position I want. Then I start building the body masses, laying the clay on in the shape and size of 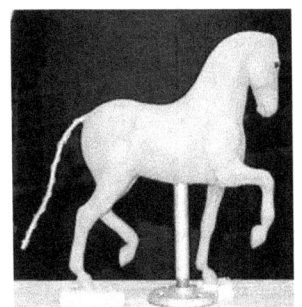 the musculature whenever possible. The horse will soon take shape from here. I use my tools and fingers to blend the clay and build its density, so there won't be any depressions from pockets in the supporting clay. You don't have to worry about trapping air in plastilene as you do with water-based clay, but if you don't build the piece solidly, bumping a spot over an air pocket can create a depression you didn't want. Build it solidly to make it strong.

When you think you have the muscling where you want it and have the piece smoothed into what looks like its final form, run a small square of nylon screen door mesh over your sculpture. This will show you dips and bumps you didn't notice visually in the clay, so you can repair them. It also helps to shine a light on the piece from the side (or hold it in your hand and hold it at various angles and distances) so you can see any imperfections in the surface. It also helps to hold the piece up to a mirror to make sure you have the proportions right. Holding it up to a mirror gives you an amazingly different view of the piece.

Here are a couple of trade secrets – you can use ball earrings or taxidermy eyes for your animal's eyeballs. Having a hard surface to work against makes it easier to do expressive eyelids. And if you want to have a flying tendril of hair, stick a wire into the body of the horse to support that bit of clay.

After you've finished sculpting and the piece is ready to go to the foundry, you can use any citrus-type liquid cleaner and a small, soft brush (such as an oil painting filbert) to get crumbs off and help smooth the surface.

Above is the getting-close-to-finished horse from "Elegance" – notice the wrapped armature wire showing where his tail will be. The finished clay of this horse is shown on the next page. The "unfinished" parts of the harness and bridle will be made from copper wire during the metal chasing and fabrication part of the bronze-making process.

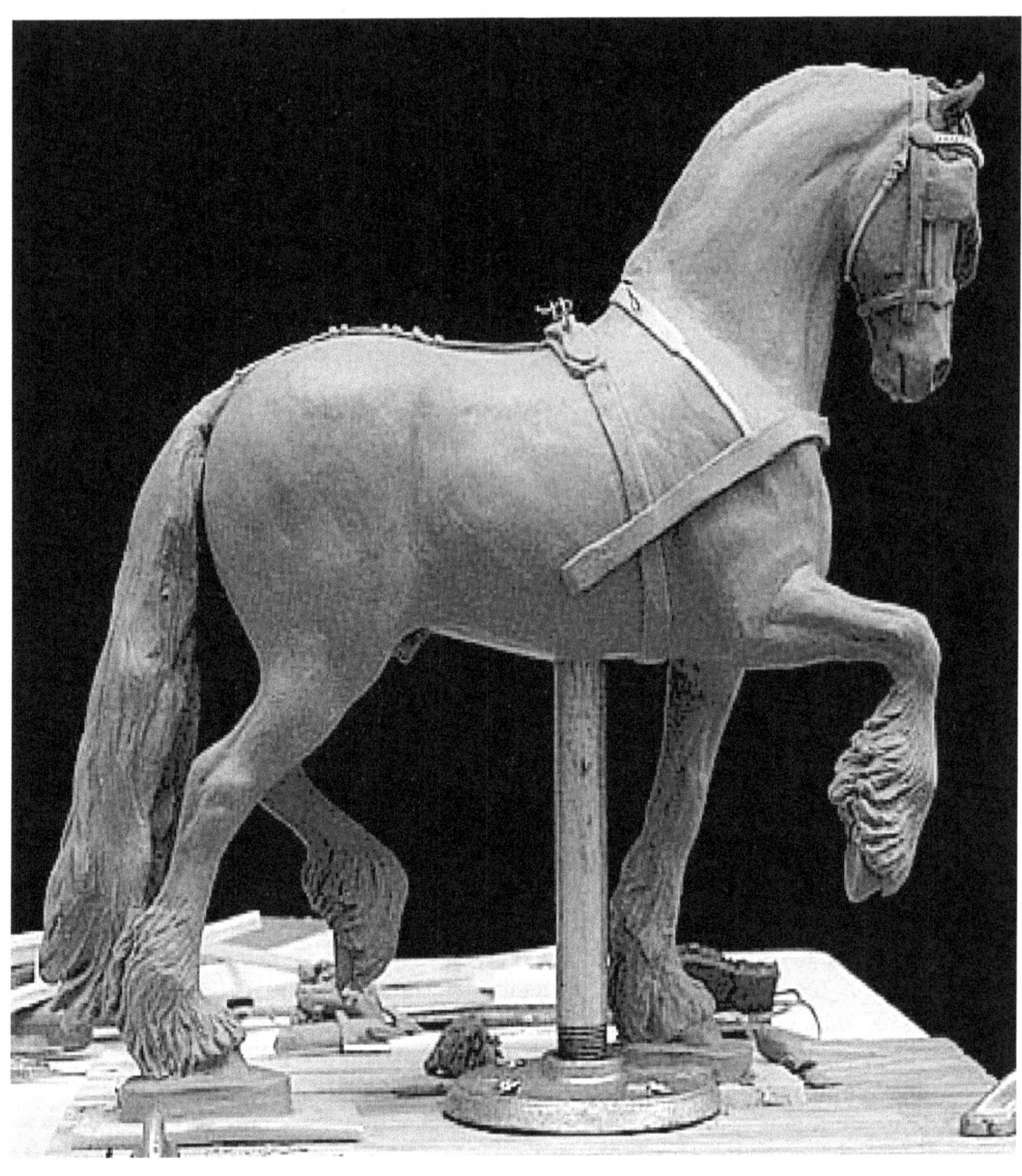

Finished clay of "Friesian Elegance" © Lynda Sappington

The finished bronze of "Friesian Elegance" is on the next page. You'll read more about this piece in Chapter 6, starting on **page 41**. The horse is black, the carriage black with red cushions and gold (buffed-back bronze) trim, the wheels, undercarriage and shafts a pale silvery color to represent white, the man's clothing is black, his shirt silvery-white, and his socks are a very pale silvery blue. The horse's browband has red on the "leather" part, and the chain decoration has been buffed back to pure golden bronze. The base is walnut.

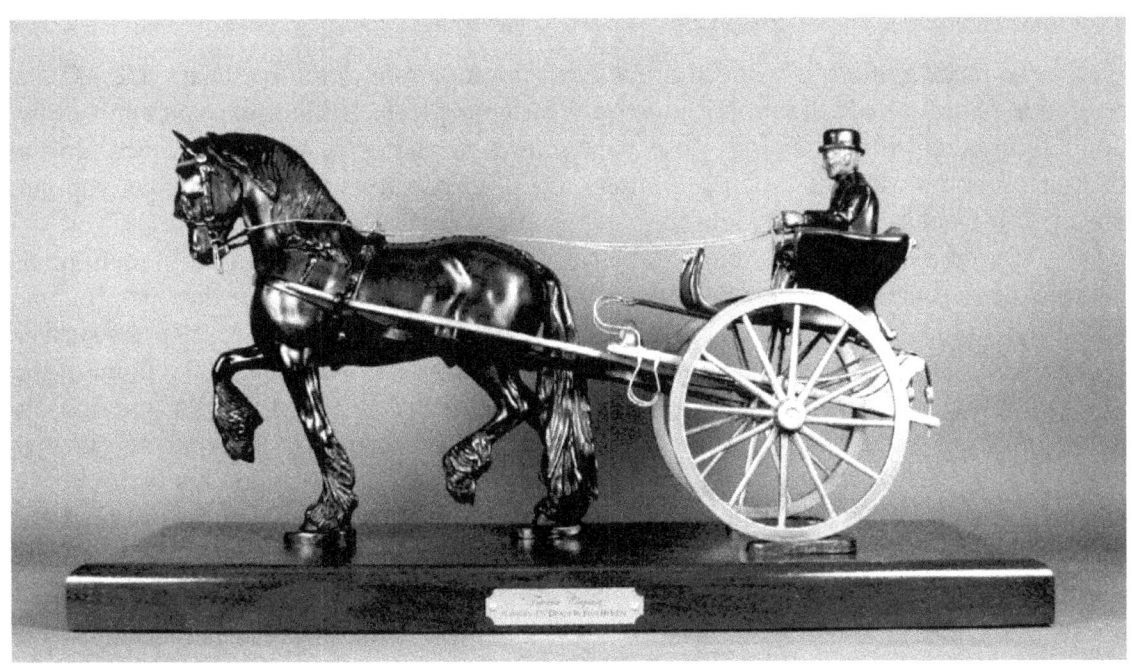

"Friesian Elegance"

Signing Your Work

You should always sign your work when it's finished. Sign with your name and the © (copyright) symbol (which automatically copyrights your work). Adding the year isn't necessary to protect it, but some artists do like to put the year on their work (I do). Be sure to carve your name and the © deeply enough that it will be easy to see after the piece is cast. I usually sign my work on the base (whatever's supporting the horse) or some other unobtrusive place. For reliefs, if there is no "ground" under the horse, I'll sign my name along the back of the horse's buttocks – really, wherever you can find the room and that looks good to your eye is fine.

Reliefs

Reliefs are fun. They don't require armatures, they're easy to make molds off of and cast yourself, and they aren't expensive to reproduce in resin or paper. You can do extremely low reliefs (such as you see on a coin) or very high reliefs that are nearly three-dimensional. Reliefs can be small and mounted in a picture frame (like "Extend" at right) or large and hung unframed.

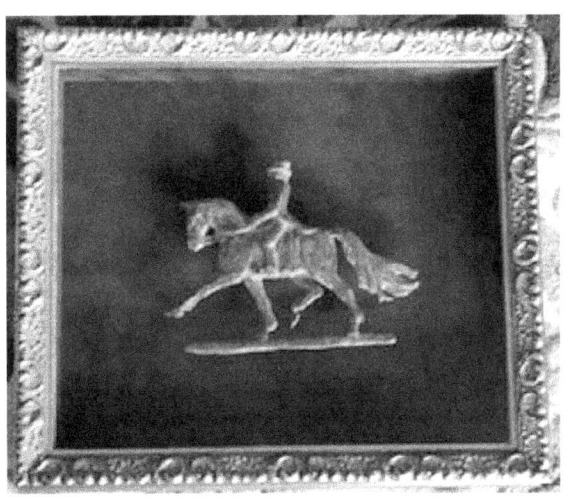

To make a relief, if you can draw, draw out a picture to go by. Use some of your reference photos to get the proportions right on your piece. If, like me, you can't draw, don't think about it as drawing – use your reference photos to sculpt the piece, do the measuring you always do when sculpting, and just keep it as "low profile" as you can manage. It's not as hard as it looks.

If your piece includes reins, as "Extend" does, you will need to build them up to the thickness of the whole piece – you can't leave space behind them or they won't come out of the mold. Also, they need to be wider at the back edge than they are on the surface to unmold as easily as possible (so the mold is releasing a "V" shape with the point of the "V" being the actual rein surface you see. The rest of the "V" won't be very noticeable to the viewer – you can't really see it in this picture, can you?) This "V" idea is important to remember for all of your edges. You can't have any undercuts in a relief or you won't get it out of the mold intact. Every edge needs to be beveled as it reaches the working surface. Keep that in mind.

You can work on any surface. I work on wood, glass, foam core, scraps of matboard, whatever's handy. You can work in plastilene, polymer clay, water-based clay (and you don't have to fire the piece to make a mold on it), whatever you want that you can get to unmold easily. Once you get your sculpture done, clean it and your working surface up. The mold you make will include the working surface, so you want to be sure the working surface has the texture you want – clean and smooth, wood grained, or textured however you want, but clean of sculpting debris.

Measuring

As they say in carpentry and sewing, "measure twice, cut once" and you'll save yourself a lot of headaches.

It's best if you make up a chart with a profile and frontal sketch of whatever your subject matter is, human, horse, whatever. There are particular places you need to measure to get the proportions right in three dimensions, and you can't always get this information from photographs. So buy a long tape measure, a good caliper, a clipboard, and a calculator – they are all sculpture tools too!

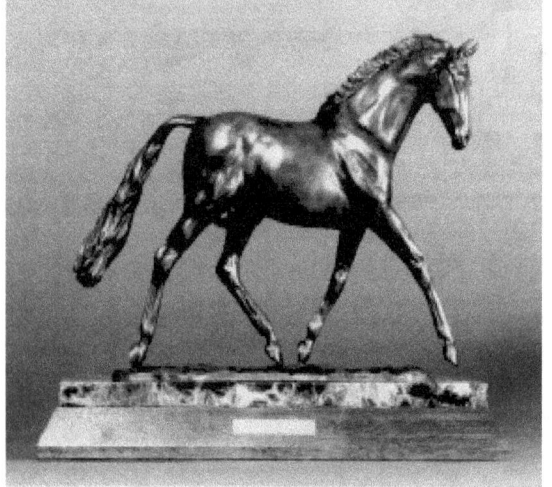

Make up the charts with lines on your drawing showing where you want to measure. Number each line, and then make a list of numbers with TWO blanks behind each number. The first blank is for the actual life measurement. The second blank is for your reduction figure. Using the decimal system side of your tape (centimeters instead of inches – that makes the reduction math easier), measure the important parts of your subject and note the "real life" measurements on your chart. (My chart is Appendix 1 in the back of this book to get you started.) When you've measured all the parts you feel you need as references, get out your calculator and start figuring. If you want to make a sculpture that's 1/8 life-sized, for instance, like "Presence" (above), divide each of your measurements by 8 and note that number in the second blank on your chart. Don't worry about taking too many measurements – better to have more than you need than not enough, and with experience, you won't need as many specific measurements.

Working Method

Turn the work frequently, work on various sections, not just "front to back" or anything like that to avoid any part getting out of proportion. Try to build up the entire piece equally, and check in the mirror to look for disproportionate places.

On the next page is a list of "Comparative Measurements" I keep on my studio wall. Feel free to copy it and hang it on your wall if you wish. It's based on measurements I've done of horses, as well as charts supplied in the Dover book *An Atlas of Animal Anatomy for Artists* by Wilhelm Ellenberger, edited by Lewis S. Brown. I have a lot of anatomy books and charts, but this book is by far the best. You can get it at www.amazon.com or any large book store or art supply store that sells books.

Comparative Measurements

(These measurements are close to equal, not always EXACTLY equal)

<u>1 head length</u> = depth of barrel at center of back = top of croup to stifle = width of barrel = length of shoulder = length of neck = point of hock to ground (see chart on following page for more specific measurements that are approximately one head length)

Length of trunk (breast to buttocks = 3x croup to stifle (or 3 heads)

Point of hip to buttock = stifle to mid-hock = elbow to back of knee = width of body at point of hip

Breast to end of ribs = 2x length of croup (measurement above)

Elbow to ground = stifle to ground = 2x length of gaskin (point of stifle to mid-hock)

Comparative Measurements Chart © Lynda Sappington, All Rights Reserved. Purchasers of *Sculpting 101* may copy it for their own use.

The Well-Built Horse and Specific Comparative Measurements

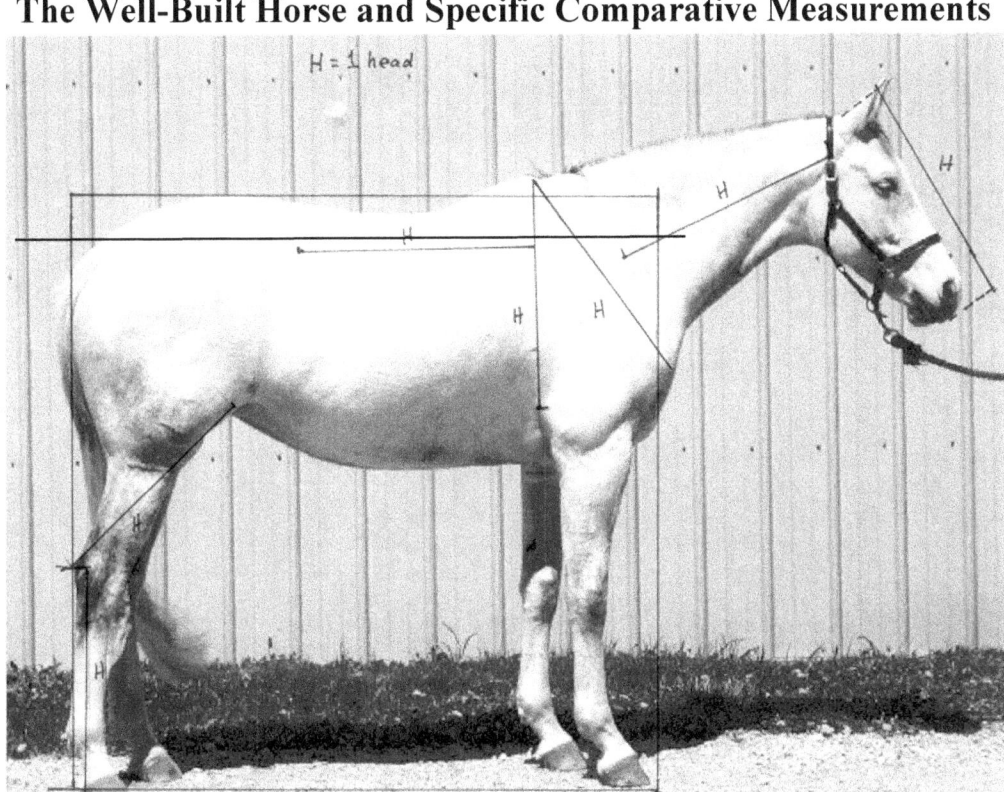

Pictured: Lydia DHF of Dancing Horse Farm, Lebanon, Ohio.
Thanks to Jennifer Truett, Lydia and DHF's owner, for posing this lovely mare for me.

A horse with good "conformation" (his build) can be thought of as a square when seen in profile (ignoring the head and neck). The length of the body approximately equals the height at the withers on most horses. A line dropped straight down from the point of buttocks should run straight along the back of the cannon bone, hock to fetlock, in a horse with correct conformation. (Lydia is standing with her leg a bit behind the vertical here.)

Well-built dressage horses, jumpers, warmbloods and others who are supposed to "sit" (work collected) are built "uphill" (with the withers higher than the croup). Race horses usually have higher croups than withers (they're built "downhill," which is best for running). The average well-built horse might have his withers and croup on the same level. The horse shown here is a warmblood bred for dressage, so her uphill build is correct for her type and use.

The measurement lines shown (marked "H") are approximately equal to the length of the head when measured with calipers from poll to lip. The measurement on the neck is from the atlas (the prominent bone at the top of the neck) to the middle of the shoulder bone. The one from the shoulder blade toward the hip stops at the external iliac (pelvis). The vertical one starting at the withers stops at the elbow. The one on the gaskin goes from the stifle to the point of hock. The remaining one on the back leg goes from the point of hock to the ground.

Notes

Chapter 4

Making a One-part Mold

The easiest mold to make is a one-part mold. This mold is flat with an open face – you can see a mirror image of the piece you'll be casting when you look at it. This kind of mold is what you use for reliefs. Any more involved casting is beyond the scope of this book, but I'll tell you how to do the open-face or one-piece mold for making reliefs.

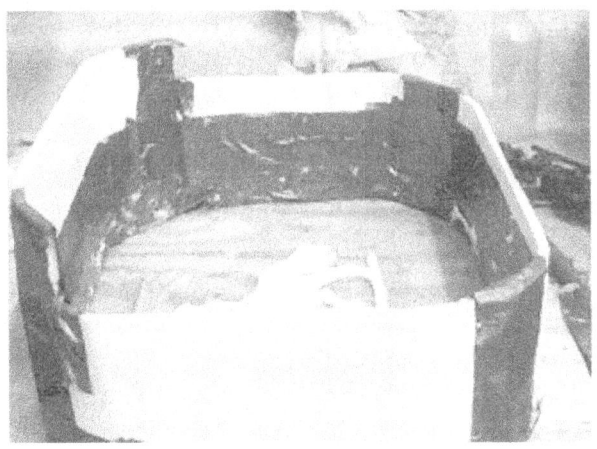

Cover your counter or work bench with a sheet of heavy vinyl or plastic. Get some foam core and cut it into strips wide enough to be about three times as high as your relief is thick (for instance, if your relief is ¼" thick, make the walls at least ¾" inch high – don't scrimp or you might be sorry about it!). Cut the strips to length to fit around the working surface (this is when it's handy if you worked on a piece of foam core to start with that you can cut to the size and shape you want the background of your relief to be). If your working surface is a lot bigger than your sculpture, simply make the box walls on top of the working surface rather than around its edges. Tape the walls in place with duct tape all around the outside. Be sure to seal the corners of the box walls with duct tape both inside and outside so they won't shift. Then use very soft plastilene clay to "caulk" the inside bottom edges where the foam core wall meets the working surface, and to seal inside all the corners thoroughly. Be sure these "caulk" lines are smooth and beveled so the rubber won't get hung up anywhere when you unmold the piece.

The mold box shown above is just an example. It's actually too large for the sculpture shown.

First, check the instructions to see what temperature the room needs to be for the material to work properly. If the room is too cold or too warm, the material will not set up properly (voice of experience again!)

Spray the sculpture, the working surface and the mold box with the mold release recommended by the manufacturer of your mold rubber. Follow the manufacturer's directions – they may suggest using a paintbrush to break up any surface tension, then spraying the mold release again. Then let the mold release dry as you prepare the mold material.

I'm not fond of math, so I prefer the 50/50 mix type mold rubber and casting material. There are a lot of brands on the market. You'll have to try various ones and see which work for you. In this example, I'm using SynAir's (www.synair.com) Pour-a-Mold 333, which is a slightly stiff, blue rubber mold material. This material is too stiff for pieces with thin, delicate places. For such pieces, you really need to use a silicon mold, which is much softer. I'll discuss them below.

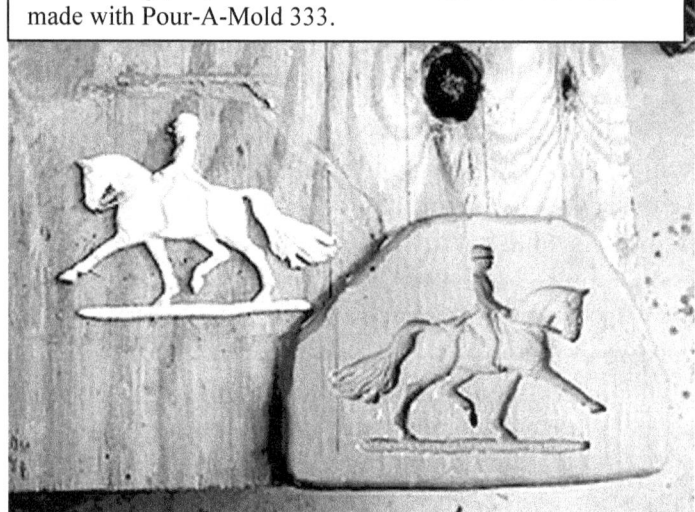

Rein casting (left) made with Pour-A-Kast Mark 3, mold made with Pour-A-Mold 333.

To cast this piece, I used SynAir's Pour-A-Kast Mark 3, which sets in three minutes. They also have Pour-A-Kast material that will set faster or slower, but the three minute setup time works best for me.

There are lots of other brands available, in both mold rubber and casting resin. Try various brands and see which one you prefer. I use silicon rubber molds now, but silicon is much harder to work with – you have to measure it in grams for one thing. Not a fun thing to do, especially for those of you who are just starting out. I'm recommending things that I've found work best for beginners here. Choose whatever material makes you the most confident in your results.

To mix the mold material, I use clear or frosted 9- or 12-oz. plastic cups I get in bulk from Sam's Club (you can also find them at CostCo, Price Club, other discount stores). There are two parts to the mold material, the prepolymer and the catalyst. I measure one part into a cup up to a line that looks like it will be half the volume I'll need. Then I measure the other material into another clean cup, up to the same line. Both cups are poured into a third clean plastic container (I use butter or cottage cheese tubs), making sure to scrape all the measured material out of the cup with a clean craft stick or paint stirring stick (something clean, strong and disposable). The mixture is stirred carefully in a figure 8 motion to avoid introducing bubbles to the mixture. Be sure to scrape the sides and the bottom frequently. When the material is an even color, it's mixed and ready to pour. This mold material gives you about 15 minutes of working time, so work carefully and don't rush. Discard your measuring and mixing containers and the stir stick when you're done.

Start pouring in one corner of the box, letting the material flow across the piece at its own pace. If you start in a corner, the rubber will push all the air bubbles out of the way and give you the best possible pour. If you pour some here, some there, or start in the middle of the piece, you are inviting trouble in the form of trapped air, which will cause bubbles on the surface of your cast pieces. Don't hurry the rubber, just let it flow, and you'll get the best possible surface.

Let the mold sit for 24-48 hours before doing anything with it (or longer, if the instructions with your mold material says it takes longer to *cure* [harden]). If the cured mold material feels firm, just barely gives to your finger and isn't sticky, you did a good job. Using a knife or razor blade, slit open one corner of your box and then peel off the foam core walls. Remove the clay from the edges, then carefully lift the mold by one corner and ease it off the sculpture. The sculpture may crack or break at this point, but now you have a mold of it so you can reproduce it! Use tiny scissors (like embroidery or cuticle scissors) to cut off any rubber "fins" inside or at the edges of the mold.

Casting

You can cast your piece in resin or paper with the mold described above. You can also cast wax in it if you want to have bronzes cast of your relief.

Again, be certain your workroom is at the proper temperature (read the instructions on your casting material's container) or the material won't mix or cure properly.

To cast in resin, you again need to spray mold separator on your mold (and on the reassembled box, if you're going to include the background in the casting). You will also need two clear or frosted 9- or 12-oz. cups and a third clean container to stir the mixture in, just as for the mold. If there are bubbles on the surface of either element of the material prior to mixing the two parts, blow gently across the surface and that will remove most of them (blowing on the bubbles does not remove them from the mold material mixture, only the resin mixture).

Pour equal parts of A and B (prepolymer and catalyst) into each measuring cup, then pour both into the large container and start stirring the mixture. Lift the mixing container and bang it gently on the counter to force any bubbles to the surface. Remember, this Pour-A-Kast Mark 3 only gives you three minutes to work, so if you feel the mixture starting to get warm, start pouring it into your mold, unless it's obvious the color has not blended completely. In that case, you need to discard the mixture, the measuring and mixing containers and the stir stick, and start over.

Again, stir gently and in a figure 8, remembering to scrape the sides and bottom of the container, and being careful not to get air in the mixture. When the casting material is completely mixed (no striations in color), start pouring into one side of the depression in the mold created by your sculpture if you only want to cast the sculpture itself. (If you're casting a horse, don't start pouring the resin in small parts like legs – let the material flow into those from pouring it into the body area of the horse.) If your material doesn't flow all the way to the ends of your mold, you can pour directly into the part that's getting shortchanged if you're very careful. If you want to include the background in the casting, then start pouring in the corner of the box, as you did for the mold.

You will feel heat coming off the resin as the chemical "kicks." You will soon see the material turning white as it solidifies (the raw mixed material of this particular brand is a golden color like pine resin). Don't try to unmold it until the casting has gotten back to room temperature. If your casting has thin parts such as "Extend" does, after you have some experience with casting resin, you can remove the casting from the mold while it's still a little warm, then flatten it on the counter to cool (back side down). If you don't do this correctly, you can stretch out your thin parts or make the piece curved or curled, so be very careful if you try to unmold a piece while it's warm.

To finish your castings, you'll need to get the surface oils off the resins. You can do this by soaking the castings in a 50/50 bleach and water mixture overnight, or by wiping with a cotton ball soaked in alcohol or by keeping the resins in boiling water for 20 minutes. You may have to sand off some rough edges. I lay the resin flat on a belt sander to do this. Be sure to clean all the dust off the casting after sanding.

To finish the pieces, I've found it works pretty well to spray the resin with auto body primer (gray or white). Then I can paint or stain the casting with no problem. If you spray them white, then dip them in wood stain, as mentioned earlier, they turn out looking like old ivory, a very nice look. If you don't spray paint them, but just dip the bare resin into wood stain, the piece will look like old ivory or bone, and will yellow as ivory does over time and with exposure to sunlight. The material doesn't seem to degrade in quality as the color changes, from my experience, but you do need to be aware the resin can get very yellow if not painted or finished. (To learn how your casting material ages, hang a piece of your cast resin in a sunny window and let nature take its course. Check it from time to time to see how it's aging. I have a piece that's painted on the front and unpainted on the back. The back is exposed to the sun through the window, and has turned a dark yellow in just a few years.)

Casting in Paper

Casting in paper is fun, and gives you some beautiful results. You can get paper casting supplies (bulk paper pulp, whatever else you need) from Twinrocker (www.twinrocker.com) and various other sources. If you contact Twinrocker and tell them you're doing paper castings of sculptural reliefs, they'll tell you which paper pulp mixture you'll need. You can buy a one-gallon "sample" bucket, which lasts a long time, or a five gallon bucket. I've never managed to use up a five gallon bucket before it spoiled, so I just buy the one gallon buckets as needed. They stay fresher after opening if you refrigerate them. Once opened, the pulp is a prime breeding ground for mold, so use it as quickly as possible after opening! If mold does form, you can kill it by adding a little household bleach to the bucket and stirring well, but that doesn't work for long, in my experience.

To cast in paper, you need your rubber mold and a loose-fitting box (foam core wrapped completely in duct tape works well) to go around it. The water needs to run out somewhere, so the box should not be a water-tight fit. You also need a sink with a strainer for the drain, a small bucket for mixing the pulp with water, a water source, and several clean cellulose sponges.

It's safest if you work with your mold down in a sink or tub, because this is a messy process. No mold release is needed. Your hands may be more comfortable if you wear rubber gloves while you're working.

Dip out a small amount of paper pulp and immediately close the bucket it came from to protect the bulk of the pulp from mold spores. Put the pulp in your mixing bucket and add twice as much water as there is pulp. Stir this mixture with your hand until it's as smooth as paper and water can get (like very loose oatmeal), then pour the mixture gently into the mold (the rubber mold with the foam core box around it). Pour until the figure and background (if you want to cast the background too) are completely covered with the pulp and water mixture. Start patting with your hand to settle the paper into the mold. <u>Pat the mixture at least three times as much as you think it needs to be patted!!!</u> Extra patting is a good thing in paper casting! Once you've patted with your hand and settled the mixture as much as possible, start pressing on the mixture with a cellulose sponge. Soak up water, then squeeze out the sponge outside the mold. Press the mold all across its surface, pressing harder and harder until you're pressing as hard as you can (it will take several passes over the entire mold to get to this point). If you see any thin places, mix up a small amount of paper and water and pour carefully in that area to backfill. Again, pat pat pat pat pat!! Then use your sponge to soak up the liquid.

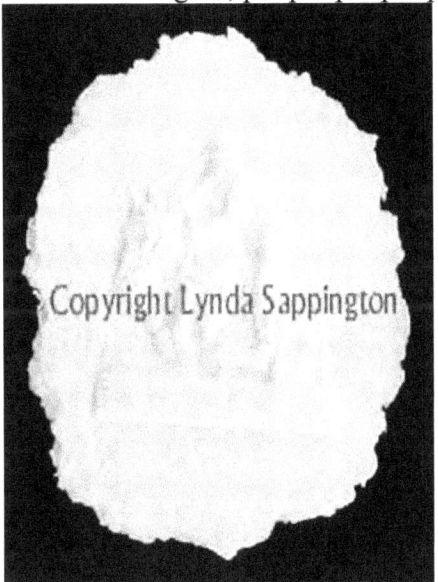

When you can no longer get any liquid from the paper into your sponge, it's time to set the mold where it can dry. It's best to let it air dry for the 2-4 days it will take a small piece to dry in average weather. You can pour clean marbles into the mold on top of the paper to keep the edges from curling. If you need to hurry the drying process, you can set a fan to blow ACROSS the mold, not down into it, and a small piece should be dry within 24 hours. You do NOT want to frame a piece that's still damp! Make sure it's as dry as possible before trying to unmold or frame it.

To unmold, remove the outside walls (if there are any) and start lifting the paper casting from one corner. If you don't like how the edges look, it makes a very pretty "deckled" look to tear or break off the parts you don't like, or you can try cutting them. The "pulp" nature of the paper will make it harder to get a crisp edge if you cut the edges. (At left, a papercasting of "Up 'n' Over" with the torn edge.)

To mount the piece, simply use framer's tape or two-sided tape to adhere the paper to small strips of foam core. It usually takes at least three foam core strips to mount the papercasting securely. Use the same kind of tape to adhere the foam core to the matboard of your frame. Be sure the frame is deep enough that your papercasting won't be pressed against the glass when the frame is closed up. *Voilà!* Simple to produce and truly elegant art!

Notes

Chapter 5

Style Points

Lines that make the eye flow around and around the sculpture without drawing the eye outside the sculpture are the basics of good artistic design. Good art, whether painting or sculpture, is full of C-curves or S-curves that make the eye travel around the piece in a pleasing way. For instance, look at "Reflection" (right). The piece is a simple C curve overall, and the bottom of the neck is also a C curve. There are C curves in various parts of the horse as well. This is a

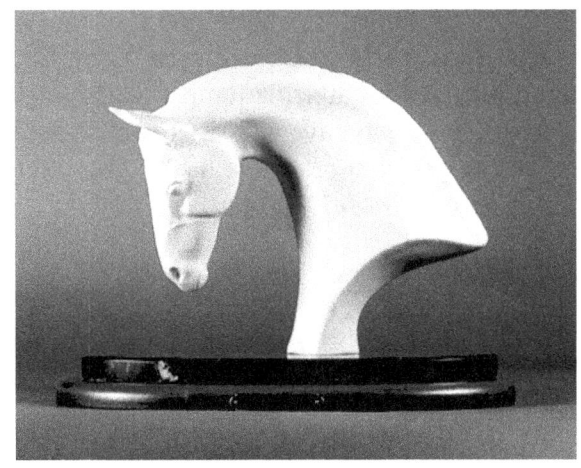

simple, graceful design that's very appealing to the eye. It's deliberately stylized instead of tightly realistic, because I wanted to convey a feeling through this piece rather than an

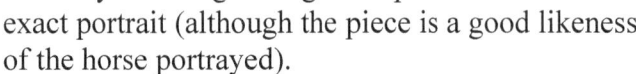

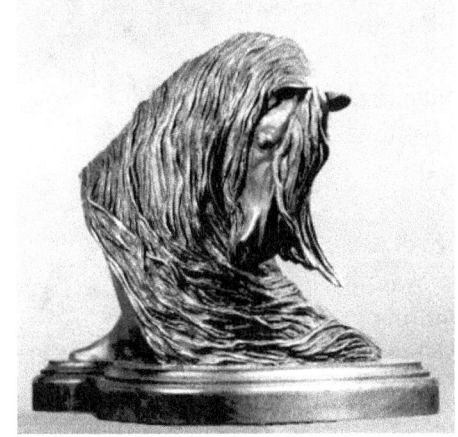

exact portrait (although the piece is a good likeness of the horse portrayed).

Take a look at "Windswept" (left). This piece is full of C and S curves. Note the reverse S curve created by the top line of his neck, down the side of his face, and along the top of the flying piece of forelock. From the top, the horse's neck is curved in a C curve. The base itself is a zigzag shape, a stylized reverse S curve. The lines of the mane from the bottom of the piece pull your eye up to the top of his neck, and then your eye slides around on that lovely S curve mentioned above. There are other curves in the picture. See how many you can find. This amount of movement makes the piece very interesting to the viewer.

Look at "Presence" (right). His right front and back legs form a C curve, as do various parts of his body. The length of his body seen from the side (nose, neck, back) forms an S curve with an extra "C" at the tail. When seen from the top, the turn of his head combined with the turn of his tail creates another C curve (both are turned to his right). His flying mane is in the form of an S curve when seen from the top or back (which is actually the way manes move in the wind). I try to find as many ways as possible to incorporate C and S curves into my work. (Look for all the S and C curves in the other sculptures in this book.)

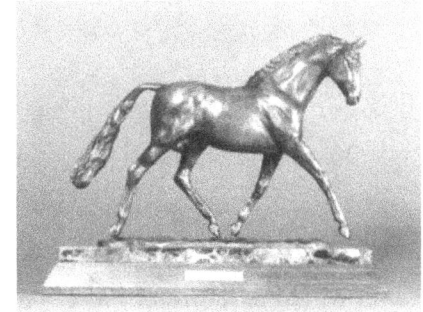

Sculptures with three or four connections to the base will be strong and stay in the pose you created. If you sculpt a horse standing on two legs, it will need bronze rods inside his back legs to give added strength and stability. If you put a horse on one leg (such as a galloping race horse), you're asking for trouble, since bronze is a soft metal. It may bend in shipping or if someone presses on it too hard while cleaning it. If you must build a sculpture that's only on one foot (or one that's flying, such as a racehorse in the flight phase of his stride, or a jumper), you'll need to attach him to something sturdy to support him. Don't attach a jumper to the jump by only his front feet or back legs, or he will sag. Be sure to have a bush or something brushing the rider's boot in addition to his feet touching the jump, or else have a broad attachment to another horse, for instance, to help support the horse's weight.

Bases

When I was starting out as a sculptor, I had a lot of trouble figuring out what kind of base would best enhance each piece (it does get easier with practice, I promise!). One tricky part about choosing or designing a base is that it needs to enhance and "present" the sculpture without drawing attention to the base. The base is a "pedestal" of sorts, and should not be the first thing the viewer notices. I've seen some sculptures where the base was more eye-catching than the sculpture, and I'm certain that wasn't the artist's intent. So I strive for a base that "presents" the sculpture but doesn't draw the eye away from the sculpture.

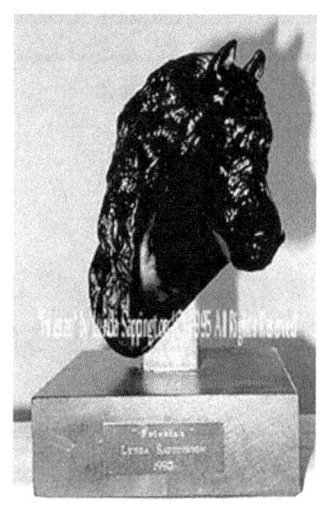

I've used various kinds of wood and marble over the years, and have learned that for most of my pieces, walnut with a dark walnut stain is best. There are a few exceptions to that rule, of course. I use a quarter-sawn sycamore base for "Lazy Afternoon" (left) because that piece has a lighthearted spirit to it, and a light base just seems to fit the mood of the piece. For "Friesian" (above right) I used a cherry base. The problem with cherry is that it darkens over time, which is the nature of the wood. But the sculpture the

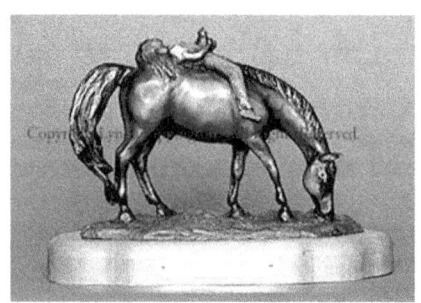

customer buys may be new, so the base is light, not the rich deep red it will become. If you use materials that will change color over time, you need to inform the customer. I love cherry, but find it more comfortable to sell pieces that will stay the color they were when they were purchased.

All my bases are custom made by my base maker, Diane Soper of Sistermaide Woodworking (contact info is in Appendix 2). The foundry can do the same for you, as well. Some foundries charge about $250 for a small marble and wood base, which is far more than I pay by getting the materials directly from my suppliers and mounting the bases with a lot of help from my husband and my base maker. When you're first starting out, there's nothing wrong with buying a pre-made wooden plaque at a craft store, staining and sealing it, then mounting your piece on it. I have several of my early sculptures mounted that way and the bases are quite suitable for those particular pieces ("Wanna Play," the black fired-clay pony shown in Chapter 3, is mounted that way). I wouldn't mount bronze on those store-bought plaques because I don't think they're thick enough to balance the visual weight of bronze, but these decisions are "in the eye of the beholder." Set your piece on various thicknesses of wood to see what best displays your piece.

Some sculptures look better with marble on the base, some don't need it. I normally put marble bases on my cold-cast porcelains and used to put it on many of my bronzes, but never on my non-porcelain resins. Busts, in particular, may need the weight of a marble base to balance the weight of the head if the horse's neck is extended (such as

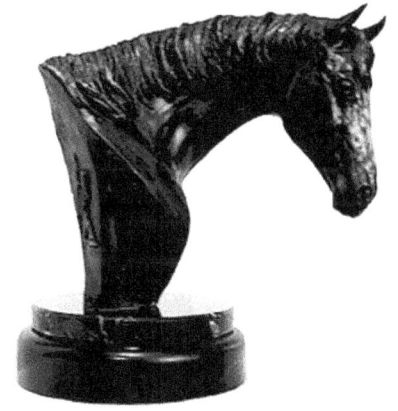

"Destiny," left, which would fall on its nose if not for the weight of the marble on its base.)

Many sculptors have their wooden bases built with a recess for the marble. On the bases where I use marble, it just sits on top of the wood – that's my personal preference. If you want your marble recessed into the wood, you need to buy the marble FIRST, then give it to the base maker to make the wooden base, unless you're using a shop that also provides the marble. Marble is often a bit off from the measurements you give the suppliers, due to the reduction in size caused by polishing the edges. To get a perfect fit, the wood has to be made to fit that piece of marble.

When choosing marble, you need to consider the color or patina of your sculpture. Black or "negro marquina" (black with white matrix) marble goes with nearly anything. Solid black marble is very elegant, but scratches easily and those scratches show up quite clearly. The fragility of the black marble surface aside, it's very sophisticated and artists along the East Coast and those who do busts and figurative sculptures seem to prefer blocks or cubes of pure black marble as bases. I prefer the warmth of marbles with matrix in them with my horses, and the varied finish doesn't show scratches very much.

Certain shades of brown marble look beautiful with liver sulphate (brown or "French Brown") patinas or certain ferric (golden brown to reddish brown) patinas. Empress green (dark green with greenish-white matrix) marble and negro marquina (black with white matrix) both look great with black or white pieces. I used Caribbean blue marble (aqua with brown streaks and white quartz crystals) for a particular piece. When in doubt, take your bronze to your marble supplier and sit it on samples of the colors you're interested in. That's how I found the Caribbean blue, which I would not have considered unless I put the actual bronze on it and saw how the color made the patinas just glow! Putting your bronze on or next to the marble samples is the best way to see the colors are going to enhance each other, or if the marble will clash with the patina, or possibly draw the eye away from the sculpture. When people compliment the marble on your base before they've noticed the sculpture, your marble is getting more attention than the sculpture and you may need to choose a more subdued color.

If a sculpture has an interesting "footprint" I might do a base shaped in a similar fashion to the footprint of the piece. For a bust, a circular or square base looks good.

For a human bust, a cube of black marble is many artists' preferred mounting. You have to design a base that's heavy enough and large enough to balance any sculpture that's naturally off-balance, like a horse bust with the horse's head at the end of a stretched-out neck, such as "Destiny," shown on the previous page. He's so front-heavy due to how stretched-out his neck is, I had to mount this piece off-center on the base to balance it. The weight of the marble helps balance a front-heavy piece like this one.

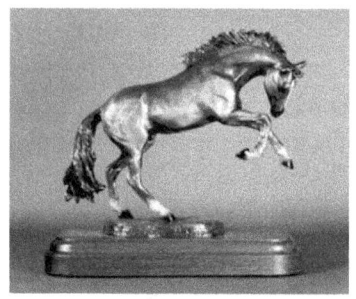

For a full-body horse sculpture, I normally use a rectangular base. A marble and wood base is considered a "western" base and is seen widely in western-style and wildlife art and in galleries throughout the West and Midwest even on non-Western pieces. In the East, plain black marble bases are preferred by many artists. I'm in the Midwest, so I do whichever kind of base pleases me (and would no matter where I lived!).

Bases can be made using just marble slabs or cubes, or just wood. I've done several pieces with just a wood base and am quite satisfied with how they look ("Lazy Afternoon," "Windswept," both shown previously, and "Frolic," shown above, are examples of my work on wood bases). The choice of wood, marble, wood and marble, a large beautiful stone, no base at all, whatever, is in the eye of the artist. You have to decide what makes your piece look its very best, then go from there.

Mounting the sculpture

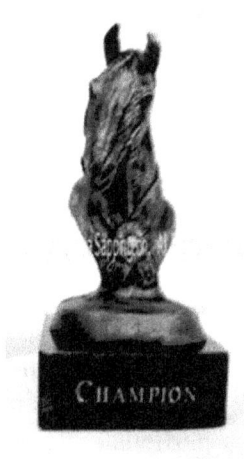

If the sculpture is a small, lightweight one, with a small lightweight base, you might be able to epoxy the base and sculpture together with no real problem. "A Good Day's Work," a resin sculpture which is only five inches tall without its base, is mounted this way. To mount a piece using epoxy, you will need to use coarse sandpaper to roughen the base just where the sculpture will sit, and to roughen the base of the sculpture. Surfaces with some "bite" make the epoxy adhere better. Make sure both surfaces are clean and dust-free, then mix up your epoxy and apply it to the center of the bottom of the sculpture. Line the sculpture up with the base and press it into place, wiping away any epoxy that squishes out immediately. Let it stand longer than you think it needs to so the bond will be as strong as possible. (A good way to tell when your epoxy is set is to keep the mixing surface you used to mix the epoxy, and check to see when that is completely set. When that's done, your sculpture should be securely mounted.)

For larger pieces, you'll need to bolt them to their bases. Bronzes are usually drilled and tapped so they have a place for you to insert a bolt or screw. (It's always better to have two bolts than one so the piece can't turn on its base. If your foundry does give you a one-bolt mount, ask them to add another, or a pin you can epoxy into a second hole.) You can also ask the foundry to provide the base and mount the piece, which adds to the cost but makes life simpler for you. I prefer to design my own bases and have a woodworker who makes my bases for me (her contact info is in Appendix 2). I get my marble from a local marble supplier (find a place that sells floor tiles and countertops – they can also provide custom cut marble and granite). You can probably find similar resources in your area. When you order marble, you have to provide either dimensions or a template for the marble to be cut the right size and shape, and they will even drill the holes if you mark where you want them.

For resins, you may need to drill and tap the resin to receive a bolt, unless the foundry has done this for you. A brass sleeve in the hole will ensure an even stronger bond than just tapping into the resin. USE A LEVEL when you're drilling the hole in the resin to be sure you're drilling the hole straight in and not at an angle!!!! I cannot stress this enough! And be sure you don't drill too deep into the sculpture (so you don't get too close to the surface of the piece). Then measure your threaded rod and cut it to length so it will be long enough to go in the sculpture and through the marble and wood, leaving room to put on a nut and washer. (When you drill out the bottom layer of base, remember to drill a large enough space for your wrench to be able to fit around the nut). Cut the threaded rod to length, put epoxy glue into the hole in the sculpture, and epoxy on the end of the threaded rod. Screw it in, and let the glue set long enough to be certain it's solid. Then just put the base on, add a washer and tighten the nut. Or just use bolts of the proper size if you don't want to deal with the threaded rod and epoxy.

I usually cover the entire bottom of the base with adhesive-backed felt (available by the yard in various colors from Art Display Essentials, www.artdisplay.com), but you can use felt spots or rubber feet or whatever suits you. (HINT: Felt stretches a LOT so cut it ¼" smaller than the tracing you did around the base – you did do a tracing around the base before you cut your felt, right? ☺ And don't pull the felt too hard or it will stretch out of shape.) Bare-based sculptures look cheap – this kind of attention to detail (in this case, protecting your customer's tables) is very much appreciated by customers.

Name plates are common on western and wildlife sculptures. I use them on certain pieces. On others, particularly those which have no real "front," such as "Windswept," I carve the name of the piece into the sculpture itself (in the grass, next to my signature), rather than having a name plate draw attention to one particular angle of the piece. It's up to you whether to use name plates or not. You can find name plate suppliers in the classifieds of any painter's magazine, or use your local trophy shop. I prefer to screw on name plates rather than using the adhesive-backed ones, which don't stay on bases that are not flat (such as a circular base) for very long.

Notes

Chapter 6

Some Advanced Stuff

This next lesson isn't to be entered into lightly. Making a carriage is difficult at best, and they're very costly to produce at the foundry. But if you should find yourself needing to make one, at least you have instructions to help you get started! For your own sake, though, don't try this until you're very confident in your skills or you may become much too frustrated.

This Particular Carriage

Carriages come in many forms, which makes giving you specific "how-to" instructions a bit difficult. I'll tell you how I made the Friesian *sjees* (pronounced "chaise") for the Friesian Extravaganza World Championship *Concours d'Elegance* trophy in 2007, which was commissioned by Scott and Shelley Kelnhoffer of Fenway Farms, Hortonville WI, who own the lovely stallion Nanning 374.

Normally, when I portray a horse, particularly if his tack is unusual to me, I want to see that horse in person and take proper measurements and photos to make certain I will capture him and his tack accurately. But this horse and carriage were many states away and the project was kept under wraps because it was meant as a surprise to honor the man driving the carriage, Fred Hekstra. I was sent a collection of photos that were so high-definition, I was able to print them out at 11x17 (A3 paper) on my Epson 1270 color printer with no loss of quality at all. I was also aided by Fred's son, David, who went to Fred's farm to take detailed photos of the carriage when Fred was away from home.

This type of carriage is based on a Dutch style first seen in the late 18th-century. This particular carriage was built by Fred Hekstra. Like other such carriages, the shafts are not the same shape, and they are mounted on the carriage so the horse winds up off to the right, rather than centered, as is true of most single-horse carriages.

Enough background – on to the task at hand!

Putting the Horse before the Cart . . .

As I'm doing with "Horseplay," I built the horse and carriage on two separate bases, then set them up together as needed. I also shipped them to the foundry separately. I'll show you how I shipped them in Chapter 8.

My first decision was how large to make the piece. Since it was to be a trophy that would be carried into an arena to be awarded, it had to be small enough to be carried easily, but because of the fine detail of the carriage and the horse's harness, it also had to be big enough for it to be possible to make those details. I decided 1/10th life-sized was a good way to go. Nanning is 17 hands tall (for you non-horse-folks, there are 4 inches to a hand, and the measurement is taken at the withers, that bump on the back that's at the end of the neck), so I did the math and came up with his size. Since I've sculpted quite a few

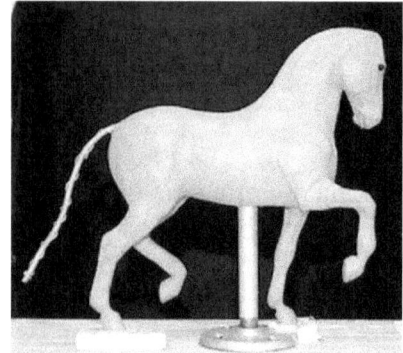

Friesians (and a lot of other horses), working out his proportions based just on the photos I had wasn't too difficult. Here he is at an early stage. (His feet are on pieces of Styrofoam to raise him to the height I needed for the carriage).

Once I had him about this far along (built to measure, but still rough on details), I was able to start building the carriage. I was provided with measurements along with the detailed photos of the carriage, so I worked out the scale for the carriage.

The Carriage

I needed to mount the carriage body in mid-air so I could build the very open undercarriage separately. The way I mounted the carriage body was quite secure, although it looks delicate. I measured to see how far behind the horse the carriage body had to be and marked that spot as the front edge of the carriage. Then I measured to see how high the carriage body had to be. I drilled three holes in the working surface, put countersunk holes in the bottom of the carriage's working surface (a board with nothing on it at this point) inserting threaded rods through them and attaching them with nuts above and below the working surface so the rods wouldn't shift. Then I used bass wood and balsa wood to build the carriage body (bass wood is stronger than balsa – I used bass for

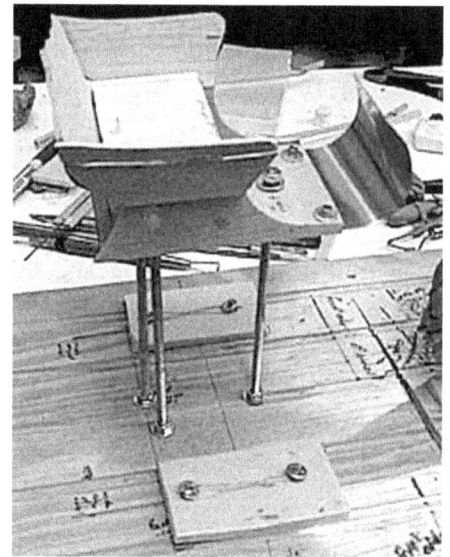

the wagon seat and the floor since it had to bear weight, and it wouldn't deteriorate like balsa would from friction against the threaded rods as I worked on the piece.)

The rectangles on the working surface to either side of the threaded rods are thin pieces of foam insulation board I used to raise the height of the pads that I built under the wheels so they'd be even with the horse (note the pads under his hooves in the photo above). I built pads under the carriage wheels so there would be enough bronze to allow a secure mounting to the base, because the wheels are so narrow. These pads also gave me a place to sign the sculpture. My signature, the piece's title ("Elegance") the copyright year and edition number are around the edges of the pads under the wheels. I added pads under the horse's hooves for visual balance – his hooves are big enough that they would've be fine to screw into when the piece was mounted on its base. The screws you see on top of the wheel pads hold armature wire that was figure-8'd in place so the clay pads wouldn't move once they were put there.

The carriage floor was attached to the threaded rods with washers and nuts above and beneath it. The front rod was positioned so it wound up between the driver's feet.

The foundry cut this off in the bronze so you'd never know it was there. The other two rods end in the opening under the carriage seat.

The carriage back and sides were made of balsa wood. The sides and back needed to have graceful curves, which would be created in clay. The shiny thing you can see on the outside of the carriage is a copper wire stretched from one side, across the back, to the other side, to support these outward-leaning pieces of balsa wood. This wire was hidden once the clay was added. The balsa wood was attached with a special model-maker's glue that dries quickly like Super-glue.

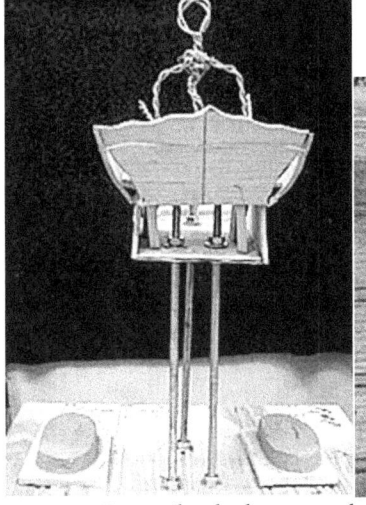

The dashboard was made of a sheet of copper made to do copper punch or relief crafts. I found it at a craft store, cut the piece to size, then wrapped it around a piece of PVC pipe to get the proper curvature. The copper sheet was attached to the basswood floor with pop rivets (my hubby's idea – he's a genius!).

At left, you see the carriage with the armature for the driver installed. I put two screws in the seat (see top view below) and wrapped wire around those to anchor this armature so it would be sturdy.

The angle of the carriage bed is not a mistake. The real carriage is hung on leather throughbraces (straps used as springs). It rocks back with the weight of a passenger. The angle shown reflects the weight of the driver in the seat.

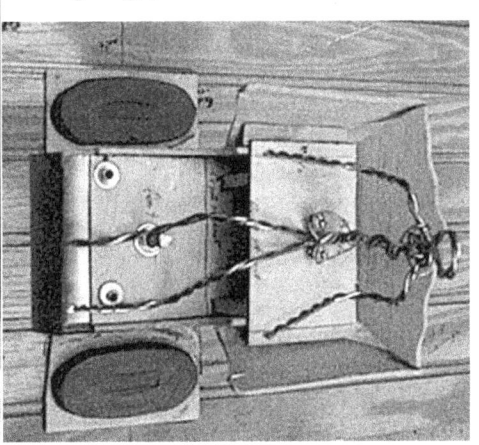

Note the wheel pads are now in place. Note also the markings on the working surface – I marked where different parts should fit in, based on the measurements I had.

I cut the balsa wood so the back edge of the sides curved the way the back should be, but the back itself is straight. Clay will make the difference.

The picture above left shows the carriage from the back, with the bottom panel not attached yet. Here you can see the gaps where the sides and back don't come together. Putting clay on took care of that. The picture's a bit crooked – the carriage itself is straight. Note I added small wood blocks under the seat to make certain that piece of bass wood would support the weight of the driver. Also note the grooves in the wheel pads, which I put there with the wheels themselves (more on them later).

These carriages are very ornate, as you can see from the carvings at the bottom of the back of the carriage (below). I carved the balsa wood with an Exacto knife and lightly sanded the edges to smooth them before putting on the clay. You can see in this photo that I've written something on the bottom panel. That's because I cut all the pieces for the carriage before trying to assemble it, so I marked what each piece was to avoid confusion.

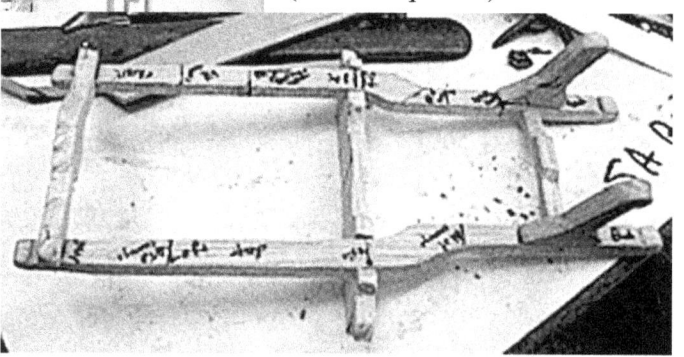

Once everything was assembled, I started putting on the clay. I'm using Classic Clay here, the soft texture and tan color, which is what I use most of the time. I built up the shape of the carriage and seat, getting the seat, in particular, as complete as possible before starting on the driver. It was difficult to get the clay to adhere to the copper sheet. I scratched it up a bit with sandpaper to try to give the clay something to bite into.

On the right, you see the nearly finished carriage and driver. I still have to add the driver's hat and hands and do more detailing, but you can see the curvature of the carriage sides now, the softness of the seat, and

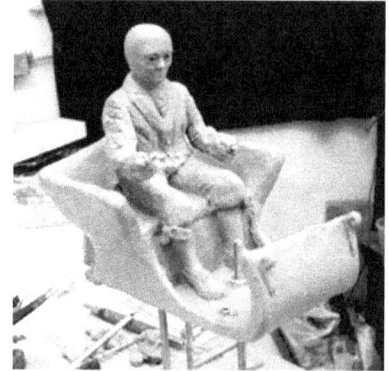

the ornamental things that are attached to the carriage. Fred is wearing traditional Dutch garb here, which is why he's in knickers (or "knee pants").

The second picture on the left is the back view of the nearly-completed carriage. Note how the sides and back have a graceful curve, with no evidence of the "gaps" that actually exist between the pieces of balsa wood. There's an ornament at the top left of the back. The matching ornament hasn't been put on the top right yet.

Above is the undercarriage. The front is to the left, the axle is the thick piece near the center, and the back is the side with the raised up things to the right. Those "raised up things" will support the back end of the leather throughbraces, which attach to metal things inserted in the bottom rails – you'll see when you get to the picture of the completed sculpture (shown below). Each piece was made of balsa wood, carved with an Exacto knife and sanded. They fit into each other via notches, which is how the real undercarriage is made. I attached the carriage parts with straight pins, because I needed to take it apart to fit it around the threaded rods holding up the carriage body. Small holes were drilled in the ends of the axle to take the toothpicks that act as the actual axle for each wheel.

The markings on the undercarriage show where various other parts fit in, such as where the edge of the carriage body should cross the front-to-back rails, etc. It took several tries to get these parts exactly right, which was true of the shafts, as well.

The undercarriage was assembled under the carriage body numerous times to make certain it would fit properly. Once I was happy with it, I covered the whole undercarriage with clay and carved in the decorative details that show in the real carriage as much as possible.

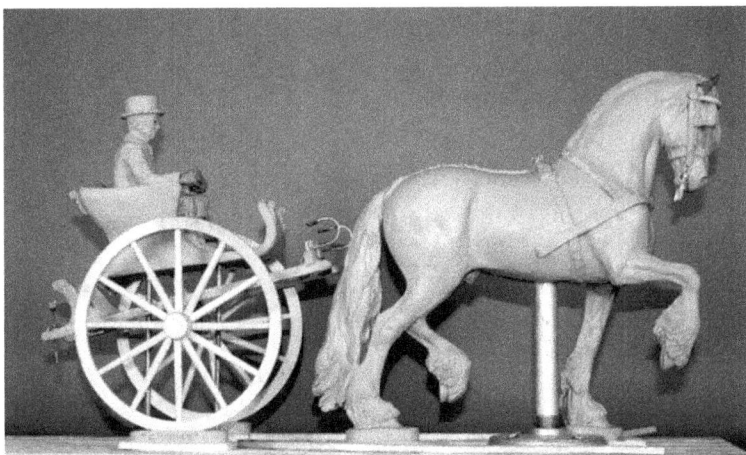

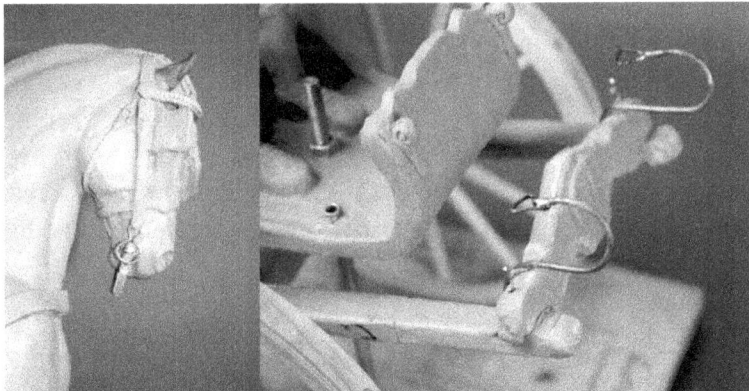

Here's the carriage with all its parts in place except the shafts (which had to be done separately). The horse has his bridle, collar, the front part of the traces (the side parts that attach to the carriage), saddle and crouper all sculpted in clay. The rest of the harness was made of wax strips that were never attached to the original horse – they were attached in bronze. The chain on his browband is part of a silver necklace I bought at a craft shop for this purpose. The metal pieces you can see at the front and back of the undercarriage are the holders for the leather throughbraces. (Front detail shown above.) I made them of copper wire, then soldered together the parts needed. There's also a step into the carriage made in copper that doesn't show here because it's supposed to be attached to the shafts (which aren't in this picture). The horse's bit is made of copper wire (for the rings) and flattened copper wire for the shanks. I wrapped a U-shaped piece of wire around the bit to have a two-pronged part to insert in the horse's mouth so the shanks would hang at the proper angle.

The wheels are real wooden wheels (six inches high) made by my basemaker, Diane Soper of Sistermaide Woodworks, Lewisburg OH (www.sistermaide.com). She makes reproduction spinning wheels as well as my sculpture bases, so I asked her to make the wheels for me. She got them accurate even to having the inner and outer hub shaped differently, just as they are on the real carriage, and she cut a groove around the outside of the wheel to show where the rim was.

Another way to make wheels is to make them of foamcore and toothpicks. You cover the foamcore parts (the wheel rim and hub) with clay and use toothpicks as the spokes, then make them look right by the way you apply and carve the clay. I'm glad I used wooden wheels – even the grain shows a tiny bit in the bronze, which makes them look fantastic.

The throughbraces, traces, driving lines and other small parts will be fabricated by the metal shop guys at the foundry, as will many of the small metal pieces shown here (many of which are too small to cast except by jewelry casting).

I made some pieces of the harness out of sheet wax, but found it was too hard to cut it accurately (in a straight line – I have trouble cutting anything in a straight line, actually ☺), so I did the harness that lays on his body in clay. If you look at the top of his bridle from the front (right), you'll see it looks like there are gaps behind the various straps. I actually filled in behind the straps as much as possible while keeping it light and airy looking, so it would pull out of the mold properly. His ears are a different color because I used a harder clay for them so they'd hold fine detail better. The 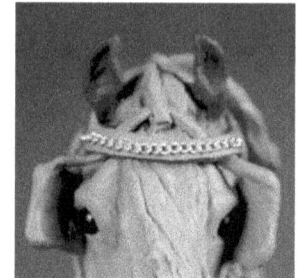 eyeballs on this particular horse are made from ball earrings, the kind that come on a card with several pairs of earrings. I also use taxidermy eyes and beads for eyeballs, depending on what size I need.

The metal chasing guys at Parks Bronze did a fantastic job of doing the detail on the carriage, even including much more detail than I could sculpt. I provided them with the large high-def photos and went there myself to supervise the finish work, and they did simply phenomenal work, even adding "nuts" on the carriage where they should be!

The shafts were a nightmare to make. They had to look like a length of wood that was square with rounded-off corners, and they had to be curved two completely different ways. I tried numerous methods to make them before my husband suggested trying aluminum rods. He used a belt sander to square them off, then softened the squared edges so they had the "rounded edge" required. I used pipe benders to get smooth curves where I needed them. With no further ado, here's the bronze of "Elegance":

"Elegance"

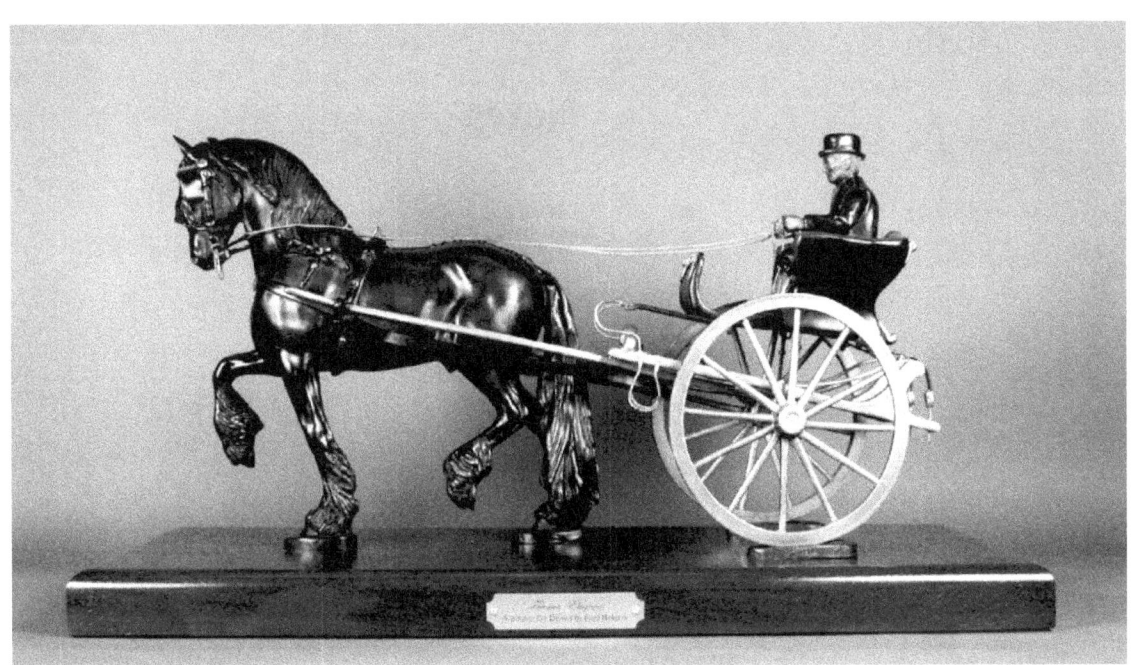

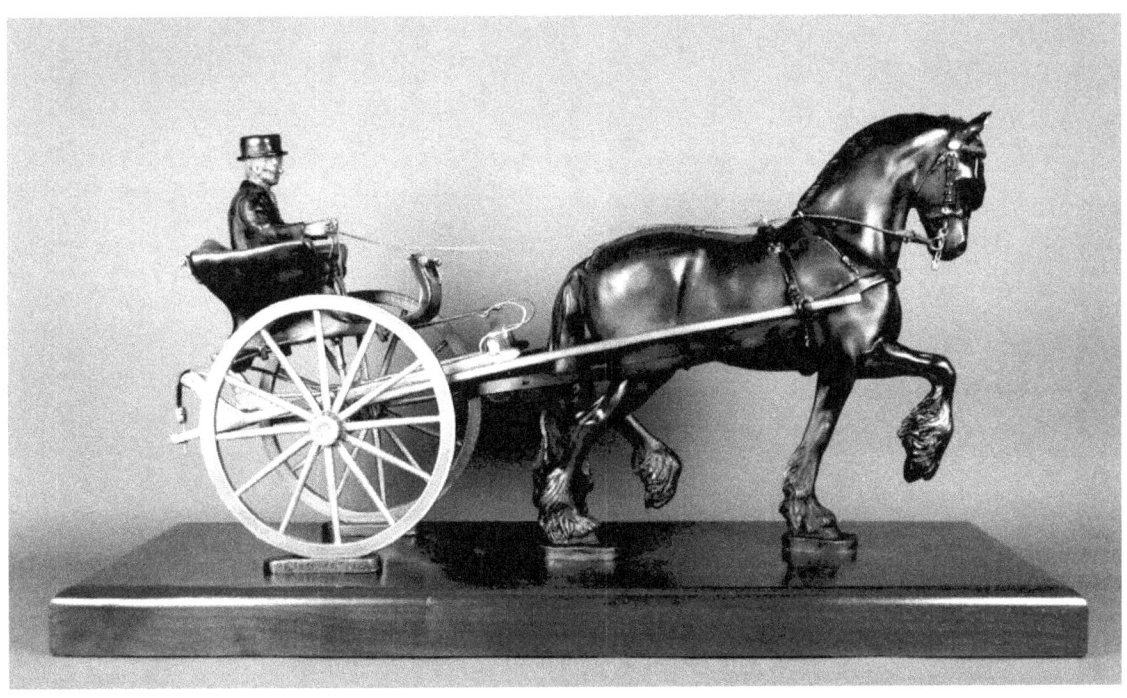

Notes

Chapter 7

Editions

You can do one of a kind sculptures your entire art career if you want to. I personally prefer to keep one of most of my pieces. In my opinion, the way to make more money with each sculpture is to do them as limited or open editions. That way, you can sell each piece at a more reasonable price than if it were a one of a kind.

Limited Editions are usually signed and numbered, and are of whatever size the artist chooses for them to be. One consideration is, how long do you want to be carrying that particular piece of sculpture? If you make your early pieces large editions (say 20 pieces), then you may be still selling some of your first sculptures when your skills have matured greatly. Most of my editions are 20 or less. Some are as small as ten pieces. A couple are editions of 50 because I believe they're going to sell quickly and well. I tried having two-year limited editions (where the sculpture is only available until a certain cutoff date, with no limit to the number of pieces in the edition) but it was a lot harder to keep up with that kind of edition. You have to maintain a list of the collectors of that piece, and notify them when the edition closes of how many pieces were in that edition. It's much simpler to set a number for the edition and close the edition when they sell out.

Some states require a *Certificate of Authenticity* to be provided with each piece sold in a limited edition. It's a good idea to provide them whether the state law requires them or not. Open editions (where the pieces are not numbered and you sell them until you get tired of that piece or it stops selling) don't require a Certificate of Authenticity.

Certificate of Authenticity

So what's a Certificate of Authenticity look like? It can be simple or elaborate, the size of a full sheet of paper, or the size of a postcard. It's all up to the artist. Basically, they need your name, studio name (if any), possibly your contact information. A gallery will usually cover contact information with their own contact info if the piece sells through them. The Certificate also needs to include the name of the piece, the number of the piece and size of the edition (#4/50 means that piece is the fourth in an edition of 50 pieces – the number "4/50" is engraved on the sculpture that accompanies this Certificate) and the copyright year. The Certificate may also describe the material the sculpture is made of, the base, any particulars about the patina, and whatever else you think is important. You can buy pre-made Certificates of Authenticity, or make them up yourself. The important thing is to make sure the information is accurate, and to supply the Certificate to your customer, or to the gallery where you're showing your work. One artist I know uses a bi-fold card for her certificate. On the cover is a picture of that piece of art. Inside the cover is "how to care for" and information about the art work. On the back is a brief artist bio. Another artist friend has a history of her type of artwork included. Others are simple but elegant post card sized cards, on nice card stock with an embossed design. The possibilities are limited only by your imagination.

Foundries

So you've created a piece you think is worth reproducing. Great! There are lots of ways to reproduce sculptures. You have to decide which one is best for your work.

If you want to produce your work in bronze, you will need to do a search online, in the phone book and in art magazines for bronze foundries that do art castings, which not all bronze foundries do. Some of them will be willing to try doing art castings for you, but they won't be able to patina the work for you, and the quality of the wax chasing and metal chasing won't be the same as it is in an art foundry. Foundries that make bronze parts for machinery do a wonderful job of producing machine parts, but it's a rare machine foundry that does art casting well – it's like comparing apples and oranges; both are fruit, both are tasty and good for you, but they're just different. So be sure you find an ART foundry!

One source for locating art foundries is *Sculpture*, a monthly magazine you can find in big bookstores. Look at the ads in there and in any other sculpture magazines you can find. That's how I found my first bronze foundry. They'd advertised in a magazine and since they were just 100 miles away from me, I contacted them. Another good way to find foundries is to ask artists you meet at shows where they get their work cast, and how they like that foundry. Sometimes an artist will have things cast at a foundry but not be as happy with their work as they'd like to be. They might continue using that foundry just because it's a convenient location or a good price, but maybe the quality is inconsistant. It's good to know these things in advance, so always ask artists who are willing to share their foundry information with you if they are satisfied with the foundry's work, and if there are any problems to watch out for.

Many artists use distant foundries all the time (a thousand miles or more away). It's harder to have creative control over your project if it's in a foundry that far away. If the foundry has a really good reputation and you make yourself clear on what you want in the finished piece, you should be able to trust them to produce it the way you want.

You have to realize there are limitations on what can be done in casting. Your finished product might look different than what you thought it would, despite the foundry's best efforts. You should be realistic about that aspect, and learn what can and cannot be done in casting. If you ask your questions freely at the foundry, they will educate you on what they can do with your piece. (For instance, the bits, reins and

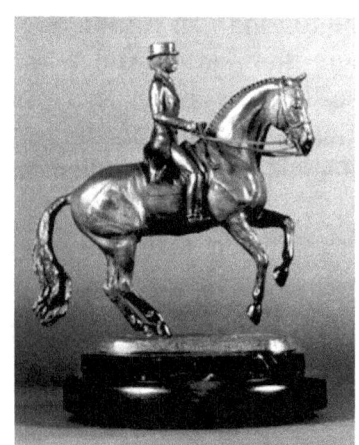

stirrups on "Harmony," shown at left, are too fine to cast – they have to be hand-made for each piece, which adds to the costs and means I have to be at the foundry to make sure they're placed properly.)

I have had sculptures cast at several different foundries. "Harmony" was cast at Tallix Foundry in Beacon NY because they had a unique "anti-gravity" system of casting bronze. The bronze was actually cast in a vacuum chamber so every little detail was as perfect as possible. With normal open pour casting systems, sometimes the tiny details like the ends of the horse's ears don't always pour correctly. When that happens, the foundry workers will weld metal to the end of the ears (or whatever else didn't cast properly) and grind it down to (as nearly as possible) what the artist had originally sculpted, or they pour a new wax and recast the damaged part, then weld it onto the bronze. I didn't want to deal with that kind of problem with this particular piece, so I chose Tallix to do this job. They were a terrific foundry, nice folks, and did excellent work, but they've now merged with the Polich Foundry and closed their old facility. I have had other bronzes cast in Indiana and Kentucky, resins cast in Kansas, and jewelry cast in New Mexico and Ohio. These days, I'm delighted to have all my bronze work done by Parks Bronze in Enterprise, Oregon. The bright, rich patinas and high-quality bronzes I get from them make it well worth the effort to get an original to them intact.

It took me years of research, asking questions, trying places and deciding if I liked their work and working with them, before I settled on the suppliers I use right now. You will need to go through the same process in your part of the country. Whenever we go on trips to other parts of the country, I check out foundries and art suppliers in that area. Big foundry areas are in New Mexico, Colorado, California, Oregon, Texas and Oklahoma. There are foundries probably in every state, but these are the states with the best-known foundries.

One great place to find out about sculpture suppliers and foundries is the Loveland Sculpture Invitational Show and Sale, and Loveland's Sculpture in the Park, both of which are the second weekend in August every year, in Loveland, Colorado. The Invitational is the largest outdoor sculpture show in the US, with over 500 artists from all over the country. At these shows, the artists are there to sell their work and you can ask them questions. There are also big sculpture supply tents with vendors for everything you could ever imagine needing for sculpting. And what a wonderful, inspiring variety of art you can enjoy there! It's worth the trip just to educate your eye about what's going on in sculpture these days. I used to do the Loveland show, but it's 1250 miles each way and we have to drive that with a truck and trailer to get the bronze there. With fuel prices the way they are these days, I stopped doing that show.

There are other sculpture shows around the country, but the smaller ones, like the Botkins Sculpture Invitational (www.botkinssculpture.com) which began in 2007 (and where you can see me and my art in person) probably won't have a vendor tent. But the sculptors there can still answer a lot of questions for you, so look for shows in your area.

Foundry Chat

When you talk with the foundry, there are some terms you should know. See Appendix 3 and Appendix 4 to learn about the process of casting bronze, both open pour and the snorkel ("anti-gravity") system that was used by Tallix.

The terms you need to know include:
- "investment" (the ceramic shell made around the wax casting of your sculpture)
- "wax chasing" (where all mold marks are removed from the wax casting made from your mold, and all surface flaws in the wax are cleaned up)
- "gating and spruing up" (a system of wax rods that are attached to the wax of your sculpture – these rods allow the bronze and gasses to flow evenly through the investment so the piece will cast correctly)

• "metal chasing" (cleaning up the bronze, removing any mold marks, cutting off and grinding down the gates and sprues to the surface of the sculpture, welding back anything that was removed for casting, grinding down weld marks, restoring any texture damaged or removed by the sprue system, fabricating detailed things like bits, reins, etc.)

• "patina" (acids and other solutions applied to the bronze by the "patineur" or "patina artist" to color the bronze the way you want it done)

Remember, the foundry wants your business. They will be happy to answer your questions, give you a tour of the facility, whatever it takes to educate you and make you a happy, regular customer. I've gotten the majority of my foundry education from foundry workers who were willing to answer my questions and explain processes to me. You can do the same thing.

Going Large

Doing life-size or monumental size work is a little different than doing tabletop size sculptures. You can make life-sized busts of people with the wooden armature shown for water-based clay, but to do an entire life-sized person, or a life-size horse, for instance, requires a few different techniques. To start with, these large pieces are nearly always done in soft plastilene if there's much detail involved, and are usually built on welded steel rebar armatures. If you want to make large, smooth abstract shapes, you can use Styrofoam boards covered with vinyl spackle or Bondo, for instance. Some artists use foam insulation over Styrofoam insulation boards to bulk up a sculpture before laying on the clay for the surface and details. Some artists use plaster instead of Styrofoam, depending on how they've enlarged their sculpture.

If you want to make a life-sized horse, for instance, normally you will make a *maquette* (small version) of your sculpture first. You work out your design problems with the maquette and get it as perfect as possible. Then you can either enlarge it yourself, or take it to a foundry to be *pointed up* (enlarged with a machine that does proportional enlargements). Pointing up can also be done manually by the artist using a grid system, or the artist can build a simple pointing up machine.

The basic pointing up machine is a long arm with a pointer at each end. The fulcrum for this arm is set at various lengths to create the proportion change (for instance, you might make the enlargement 3 times larger than the maquette). The pointer on the small end touches a point on the existing sculpture and an artist working on the larger piece will build the clay out to reach the pointer on the enlarged end. Some foundries have much more elaborate pointing up systems, up to and including digital enlargements. One way digital enlargements are made is to scan the original, and then produce slices in foam board or plaster. When the slices are assembled on the enlarged armature, the sculpture looks "digitized" in profile. A layer of clay is added, then the clay is sculpted to look just like the maquette. The most expensive type of enlargement I've heard of involves a laser that "reads" the original, then actually cuts blocks of foam material into the size and shape of that piece at the larger size. A thin veneer of clay is all that's required for such an enlargement, but to have a horse, for instance, enlarged to life size by that system can cost $5000 just for the enlargement. That price doesn't include shipping the original to the foundry, or shipping the enlargement back to the artist to finish up.

Many artists will go to the foundry that's doing the enlargement and will just stay there up to three months sculpting the piece the way they want it. If you want to do life-sized and monumental size work most of the time, it's very handy to live near a foundry that does large work.

Now it's your turn

I've given you the basics of getting started in sculpture. I didn't think I could sculpt realistic horses when I started sculpting in 1993, so I did cartoony baby dragons, little cats, etc. I didn't sculpt at all in 1994, but in 1995, I got serious and in 1996 I had to turn pro (bronze is too expensive to do as a hobby!) You may think you'll never be a good sculptor, but if you have fun with it, you're a success already!

Practice your skills by making pieces for your own pleasure in water-based clay or a polymer or air drying clay so you'll have finished pieces to enjoy. As your skills develop, you can start working in plastilene and learn about mold-making and casting if you want to. The important thing is to have fun with your sculpting. If you take joy in your work it will show in your sculptures. Happy sculpting!

"Captivating" © Lynda Sappington

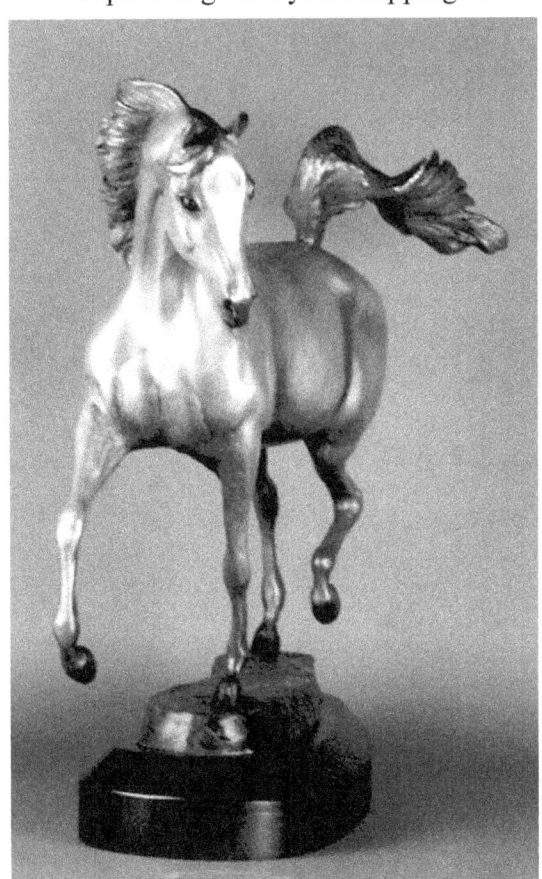

Notes

Chapter 8

Shipping your Artwork to the Foundry

One of the more traumatic things for a sculptor to do is box up an original clay and ship it to a distant foundry, hoping it will arrive intact! I've been doing this a long time now and have developed a method that works quite well.

This is when the strength of your armature is most important. It has to be strong enough that nothing will shift or sag or bounce around when the box is being handled, turned upside-down, being dropped off conveyor belts or any of the other traumas that can happen to a sculpture in transit. Another important consideration is how strong your working surface is. I found out the hard way that working on beadboard wasn't a good idea. The whole sculpture broke free of the wood and tumbled inside the box. So don't do that! Don't use beadboard, particle board, chipboard or anything else that isn't a good, strong, at least ½" thick piece of wood for your working surface.

Given that you have a strong armature, with everything fastened securely to a sturdy piece of plywood or solid wood, cut another piece of similar wood that's the same size as the working surface.

Wrap the sculpture loosely in plastic to protect it from flying sawdust and chips, then set it down into a box that allows at least two inches of clearance in every direction from the sculpture. Put your second piece of wood under the box and line it up with the base inside the box. Drill a hole in each corner from the working surface, through the cardboard box and through the outside board. Bolt the boards together with the box sandwiched between them. DO NOT USE SCREWS FOR THIS! They can back out from the vibrations the box will go through in transit. (Yes, that's the voice of experience again.)

Once everything's secure, unwrap the sculpture and make sure no chips or sawdust are on it, and that the sculpture was not damaged by you working around it. Close the first two flaps of the box and TAPE THEM TOGETHER to prevent them from falling into the box and damaging the sculpture. Then close the other two flaps and tape them shut securely.

Next, either insert foam boards at least 1" thick in the bottom and sides of a larger box, or fill it with enough peanuts to do the job (be kind to your foundry and put the peanuts in plastic bags so they won't explode all over the place when the box is opened). Slide the closed box containing the sculpture into this second box, then put another piece of foam board or more peanuts on top and seal this box shut. Then take it to your shipper (UPS, FedEx, etc.) and send it on its way.

Hot Weather Shipping

If you're shipping a raw clay to the foundry during hot weather, here's how to protect your work. Do the inside box as above, but use a larger outside box. Buy a slab or two of dry ice (look in the phone book – most cities have such a supplier somewhere) and, while wearing heavy gloves, wrap the dry ice in bubble wrap, then make a cardboard sleeve for it and slide it into the outside box next to the inside box. Dry ice will last about 36 hours, so you need to ship by overnight express if your foundry is more than a day's drive away. That kind of shipping, particularly with dry ice, which the shippers consider "hazardous cargo," is expensive, but it's better than having your clay melt off the armature in 100 degree heat, as might've happened to "Elegance" this past summer if I hadn't shipped it this way.

Special Considerations

If your piece is a complex one involving more than one element (two or more armatures, as was the case for "Elegance" and will be true for "Horseplay"), then you may want to separate the pieces and ship them in different boxes. In the case of

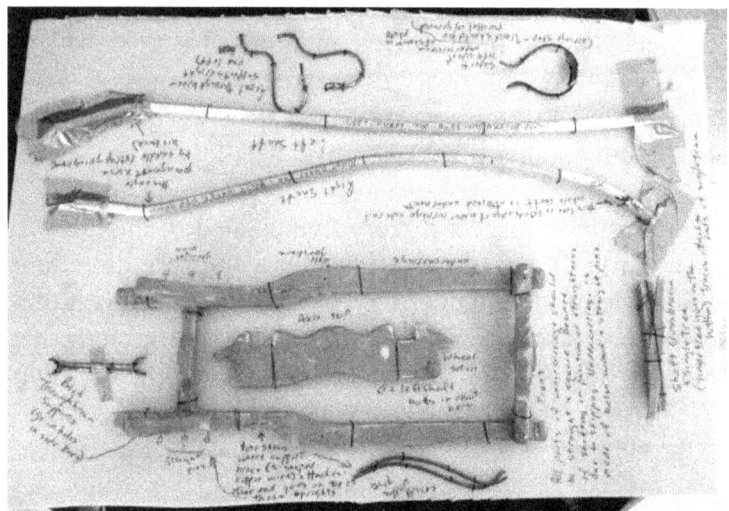

"Elegance," I shipped three boxes: one with the horse plus dry ice; one with the carriage plus dry ice; and one without dry ice that included all the undercarriage pieces, the shafts, the metal pieces, wax strips for the other harness parts, etc., and the wheels.

To ship the tiny parts of "Elegance," I actually sewed some of those pieces to thin insulation foam. Other parts were put in plastic bags and taped to the foam board.

The wheels were sandwiched between pieces of foam. All the pieces attached to foam had another piece of foam board attached above them, and then all these "sandwiches" were put in a box with bubble wrap bunched up here and there to keep the load from shifting, and shipped.

Above left you see the small parts of the carriage as well as the actual undercarriage and shafts all actually sewn or taped to thin foam board. The second picture shows the

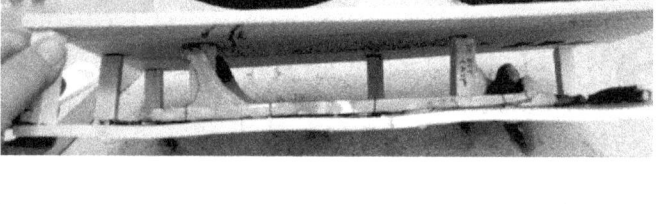

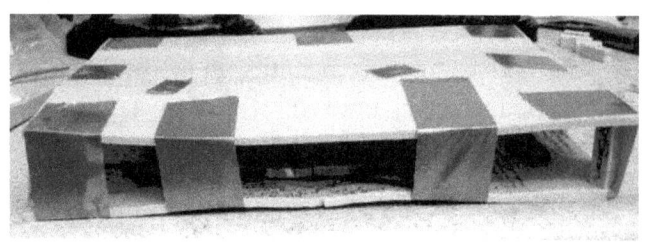

balsa wood columns I inserted (and secured with two straight pins in each end of each column) to keep the two pieces of foam board from crushing anything between them.

The last picture on the previous page shows the completely assembled package containing the undercarriage and small parts, supported by balsa wood columns and secured with duct tape.

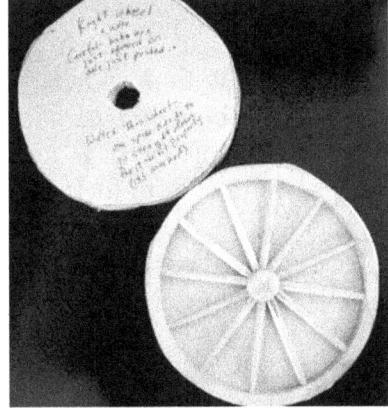

To pack the wheels, I cut a hole in stacked foam boards to cover the hubs on each side of the wheel. Then I sewed the layers together. I wrote instructions on the outside of the package, noting that this was the right wheel, the other the left, and how it had to be mounted. The bump on the outside of the package is foam board covering the toothpick that slides into the axle bar of the undercarriage.

Below left, you can see the final packing of the right wheel. Duct tape has been added to secure the package more strongly, and to hold the insulation foam over the toothpick.

The insulation foam board used here and for the sculpture itself (under the pads on the ground) is thin zig-zag insulation foam board that's made to go under house siding. You can buy it for about $30 at home improvement stores like Home Depot and Lowe's. It's useful for all

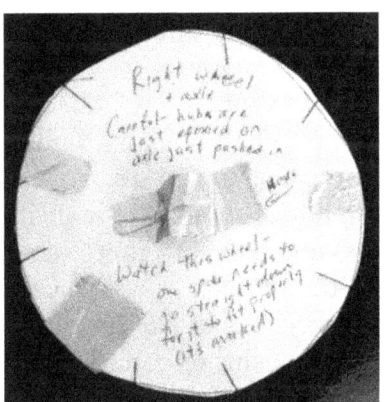

kinds of things.

Shipping Finished Sculptures

Once your piece is cast and mounted securely on its base, you may want to send it to distant art shows or to customers. It's safest to have a professional shipper pack them for you, but that's also expensive. When I ship a piece to a customer who's purchased it, I have the shipper pack it. When I ship a piece to a show, I pack it myself to save money.

Start out by supporting any fragile parts with small rolls of bubble wrap if necessary. If you have "loose" reins or driving lines, wrap a piece of flannel around them where they may touch the rest of the sculpture, to prevent scratching. In the case of "Elegance," I actually cut out a piece of flannel that's sort of horse-blanket-shaped so it lays across the horse's back under the driving lines, then wraps around his neck to protect his neck from the driving lines as well. This "blanket" is fastened to itself with a small piece of tape. Since it's fitted around the harness saddle and terrets as well as the horse's neck, it won't shift.

Once you've supported the piece as well as possible, wrap it in bubble wrap (several layers going in various directions so it's well-covered and cushioned). This is not the place to get stingy – wrap it well! Fill plastic sandwich bags with peanuts and drop them in the box, then nestle the wrapped sculpture in the box among the peanuts. Fill the box the rest of the way with bagged peanuts, then seal the box shut. Put bagged peanuts in a larger box and then insert the first sealed box. Fill up the outer box with bagged peanuts (or foam insulation board that's at least 1" thick) and seal it up. It's ready to ship!

The best professional shippers offer "foam-in-place" packaging. With this kind of packing, only a single box is necessary. The sculpture is wrapped in bubble wrap, then in shrink wrap to make as smooth and tight a package as possible. Then plastic bags are laid in the shipping box and filled with packing foam which expands quickly to lock the sculpture in place. The foam itself is soft, about the feel of a firm pillow, so it's a good cushion and easy to handle inside its plastic bag when the piece is unpacked. I've had "carry boxes" made like this to carry delicate pieces from show to show in my art show trailer.

Always insure your artworks for the replacement cost of the piece when sending it to a show. When shipping to a customer, I usually insure it for the retail price. However you choose to ship your art, make sure there's a tracking number on it in case it goes astray.

All that said, if you're hauling your art from show to show yourself, as I do, the easiest way to pack is in plastic tubs with lids. We purchased a bunch of blankets, quilts and comforters from the Salvation Army and use them to wrap the sculptures. Even fairly delicate ones ride very safely once they're wrapped up in a blanket and put in their plastic tubs. I even carry three or more small bronzes in the same box sometimes, and not one has ever gotten damaged. Delicate things like cold-cast porcelains will need more protection, and you don't want to put resins or cold-cast porcelains in the same box with any bronze. The heavier piece may damage the lighter-weight resins or porcelains.

There are lots of ways to pack art – these are just what works for me. Good luck with your shipping!

Appendix 1 - Measuring the Horse for Sculpture

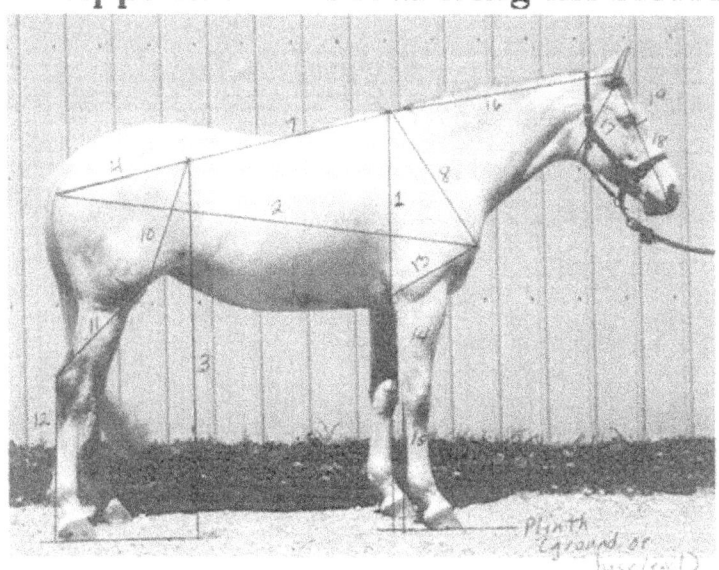

Pictured: Lydia DHF of Dancing Horse Farm, Lebanon, Ohio
Thanks to Jennifer Truett, Lydia and DHF's owner, for posing this lovely mare for me.

Line 9 should be straight from point of shoulder to point of shoulder, but I didn't draw the horse straight.

Definition of terms:

Plinth—ground or base level
External iliac—point of pelvis
    near the loin (or back)
Point of buttock—rear protrusion of the pelvic bone, a few inches below tail head
Point of shoulder—bony protrusion felt at front of shoulder
Patella—part of the stifle joint
Pisiform—bony protrusion at back of knee
Poll—pointed bone centered between the ears
Depth of head is measured with calipers from the poll to the throatlatch
Length of head is measured with calipers from the poll to the lowest point of the lip
Width of tear ducts is measured across the front of the face with calipers or a tape measure

First blank on each line is for "Lifesize" measurement (measured on the metric scale for ease of reduction). The second is for the sculpture size, for instance "1/8 life" or "30% life" whichever you choose.

Lifesize _____ Lifesize

1 Plinth to top of withers _____ _____

2 Point of shoulder to point of buttock _____ _____

3 Plinth to external iliac _____ _____

4 External iliac to point of buttock _____ _____

5 Between points of buttock _____ _____

6 Between External Iliacs _____ _____

7 Point of buttock to point of withers _____ _____

8 Point of withers to point of shoulder _____ _____

9 Between points of shoulder _____ _____

10 External iliac to patella _____ _____

11 Patella to point of hock _____ _____

12 Point of hock to plinth _____ _____

13 Point of shoulder to elbow _____ _____

14 Elbow to pisiform _____ _____

15 Pisiform to plinth _____ _____

16 Point of withers to top of poll _____ _____

17 Depth of neck at throat latch _____ _____

18 Length of head _____ _____

© Lynda Sappington. All Rights Reserved. Purchasers of *Sculpting 101* may copy it for their own use.

Notes

Appendix 2

Suppliers

Following is a list of suppliers I've used or visited myself, as well as others that have been recommended to me. This is by no means an exhaustive list. It's just a place to help you start your research. You may have good suppliers closer to you than any I've listed here. To find local suppliers, check your Yellow Pages, contact art supply stores and see if they carry sculpture supplies, or if they can direct you to someplace that does carry sculpture supplies. You can also ask sculptors you meet at shows where they get their supplies. If you find a great supplier that isn't listed, please let me know and I'll add it to the list for future editions of this book. Thanks!

Sculpture Supplies:
The Compleat Sculptor, Inc.
90 Vandam St.
NY NY 10013
1-800-9-SCULPT
www.sculpt.com

Customer Care
Sculpture House, Inc.
405 Skillman Road
PO Box 69
Skillman, NJ 08558
609-466-2986
www.sculpturehouse.com

Arizona Sculpture
Ball Consulting Ltd.
4665 South Ash
Suite G-15
Tempe, AZ 85282
1-888-967-7727
www.arizonasculpture.com
(This is where I order my Classic Clay.)

Cornell Studio Supply
8290 N. Dixie Dr.
Dayton OH 45414
1-937-454-0357
(no website, but they do have a catalog)

Bases:
Sistermaide Woodworking
6245 Pyrmont Rd.
Lewisburg OH 45338
1-937-962-4983
www.sistermaide.com

Clays and Casting Supplies:
Compleat Sculptor
Sculpture House
Arizona Sculpture
Cornell Studio Supply

Chavant, Inc.
5043 Industrial Road
Farmingdale, NJ 07727
1-800-CHAVANT
www.chavant.com

Polyform Products
1901 Estes Avenue
Elk Grove Village IL 60007
1-847-427-0020
www.sculpey.com
(Home of Sculpey products)

Art Display Products:
Art Display Essentials
www.artdisplay.com

Foundries:

I recommend you research foundries in your own area because it's easier (especially when you're starting out) to deal with one that's close at hand. There are many more foundries than I'm listing here, especially out West (Oregon, California, Texas, New Mexico, Oklahoma, Colorado, Wyoming all have good foundries I have not listed here – and there are even more than that!) I'll just list those with whom I've worked or that I've researched for possible future work, to get you started.

Bronze Foundries:

Parks Bronze
331 Golf Course Rd.
Enterprise OR 97828
1-541-426-4595
Email: parksbrnz@oregontrail.net

The Bright Foundry
1621 E. Washington St.
Louisville KY 40206
1-502-589-4337
www.brightfoundry.com

The Crucible Foundry LLC
110 E. Tonhawa
Norman OK 73069-7238
1-405-579-2700
www.thecruciblellc.com

Santa Fe Bronze
2 Otto Rd.
Santa Fe NM 87505
1-505-471-0424
www.santafebronze.com

Weston Studio Foundry
701 Airport Rd.
Santa Fe NM 87501
1-505-471-2799

Valley Bronze
307 W Alder Street
P.O. Box 669
Joseph, Oregon 97846
1-541- 432-7551
www.valleybronze.com

Polich Tallix
453 Route 17K
Rock Tavern NY 12575
1-845-567-9464
www.polichtallix.com

Resin Casters:

Spring Creek Castings
307 E. Adams
Oberlin KS 67748
1-785-475-3393

Rick Barkby
5601 Crowe Dr.
Dover PA 17315
1-717-292-1837

Papercasting Supplies:

Twinrocker Handmade Paper
100 E. Third St., PO Box 413
Brookston IN 47923
1-800-757-8946
www.twinrocker.com

To research more foundries:

The following website lists foundries all over the country – I can't vouch for those whose work I don't know, but this site may help you with your research:

www.artcastingjournal.com/foundries.htm

How Bronze is Made

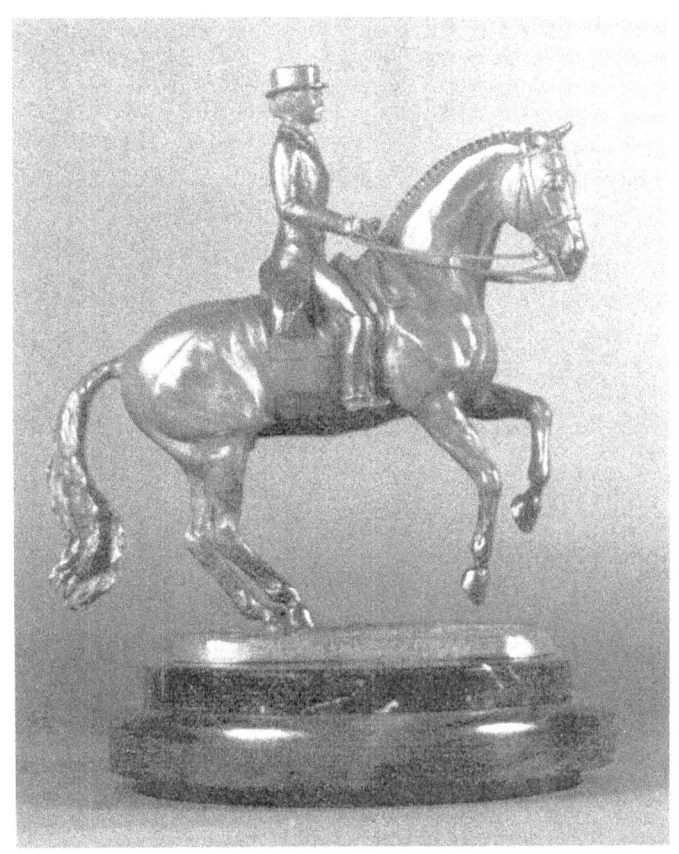

From Armature to Finished Bronze

In the Beginning . . .

The armature—pipe and aluminum wires to support the clay

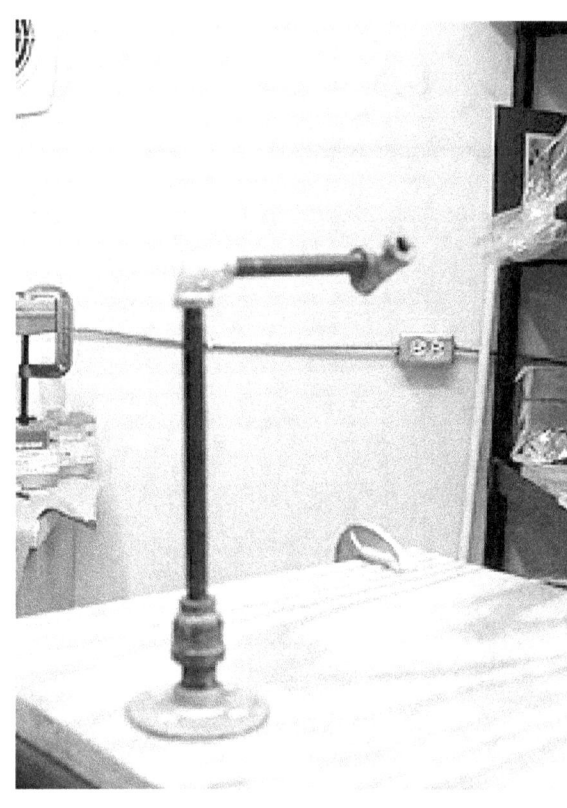

Shown: Back-iron armature

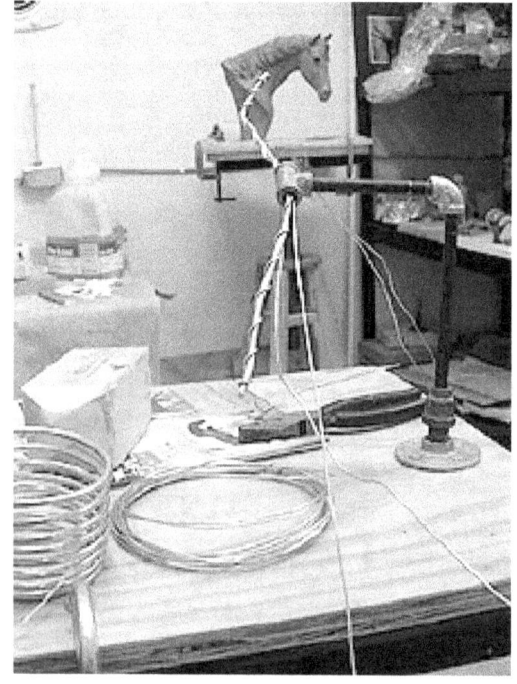

Add Clay . . .

In this case, plastilene (oil-based clay that never hardens or dries out).

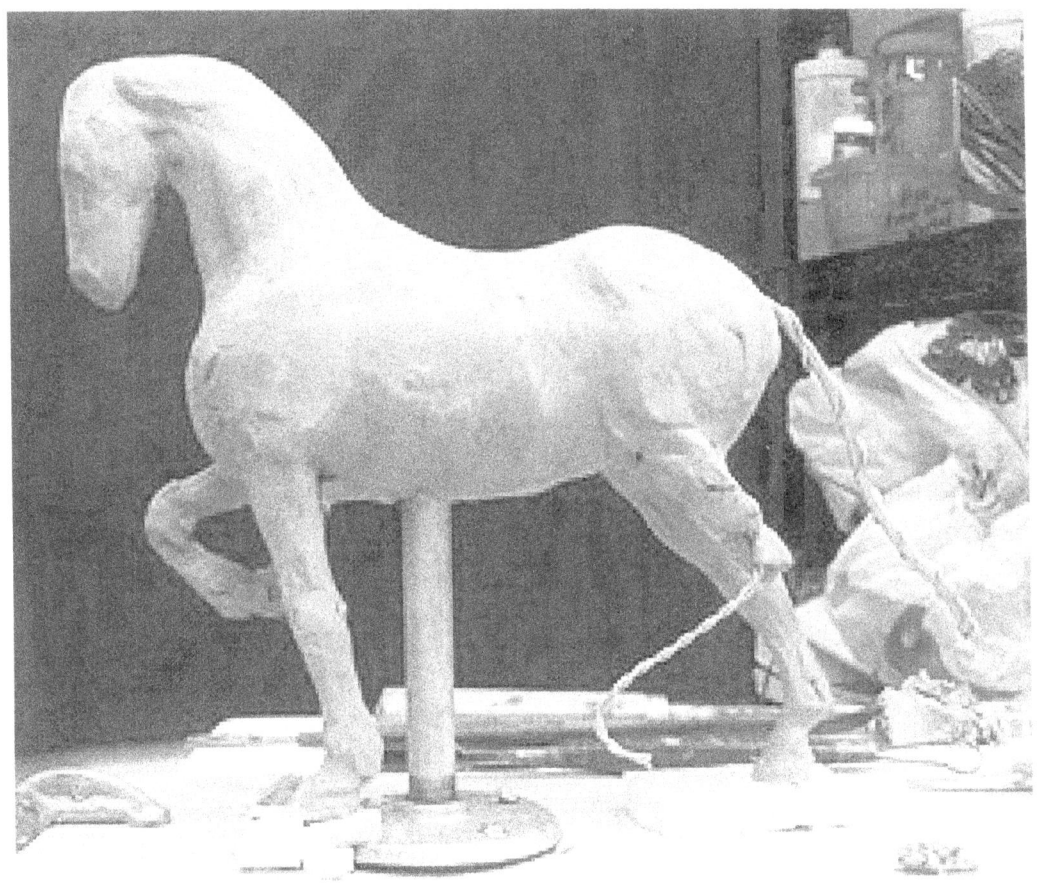

Shown: "Elegance" about 1/3 done.

Note the armature wire for his hind leg and tail.

The finished clay, ready to go to the foundry.

The foundry will make a molds of "Elegance," then pour wax in the mold to create bronze using the "lost wax method."

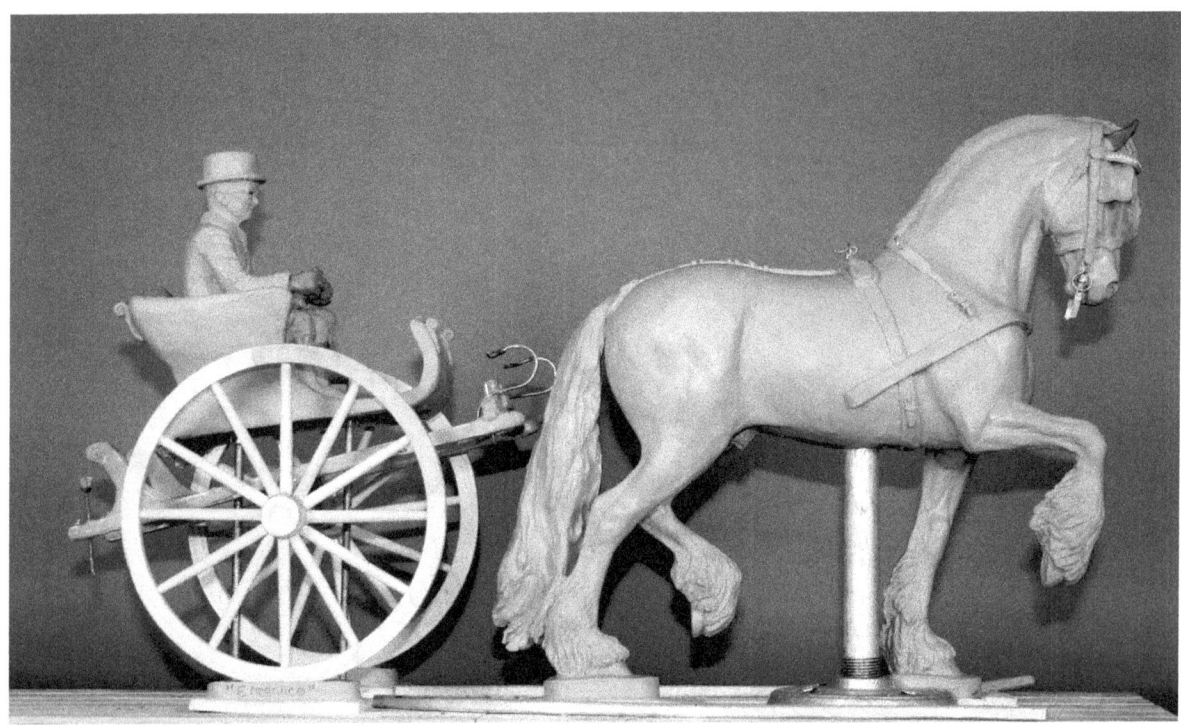

Gating Up and Spruing the Wax

The wax sculpture has mold marks, etc., removed (in a process called "wax chasing") and is made as perfect as possible. The sculpture may need to be cut into pieces to cast more easily. Most bronzes are also cast hollow, so a section of a horse's rump, for instance, is removed so the piece will be hollow when cast. That removed section is attached to the gating by a rod of wax so it will be cast at the same time as the rest of the piece. Gates and sprues (wax rods) are added to vent the gases as the bronze flows through the *investment* (ceramic shell created around the wax original) to cast the bronze. The gated up wax is then ready to *invest*.

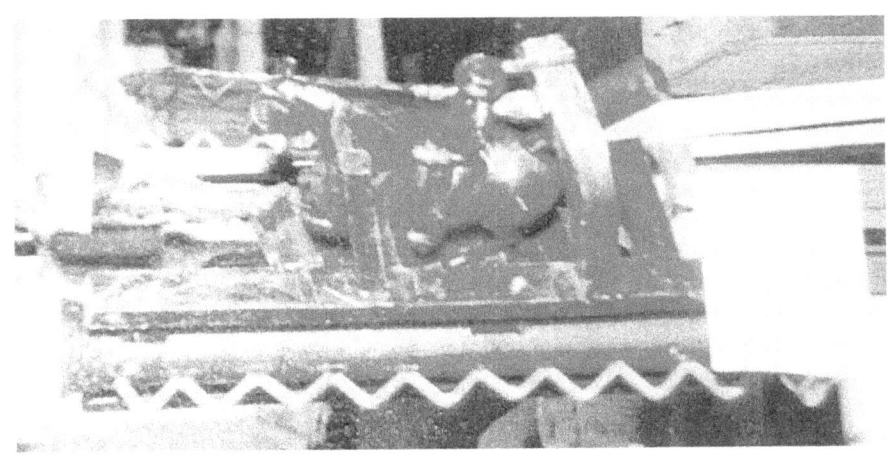

Shown above: gated and sprued wax of "Harmony."

Note zigzag wax wire which is there to let gases escape when bronze is being cast.

Investing the Wax

Step 1: Dipping in slurry

Dave Scott, of Scott Art Castings*, Indianapolis, Indiana, in his dipping room. He is dipping a gated-up wax of the front half of "Presence" with a Styrofoam^{TM} cup attached to be the pour spout. The piece is dipped in color-coded ceramic slurry. When this slurry is wet, it's green. The investment will be orange when the investment is dry enough for the wax to be burned out.

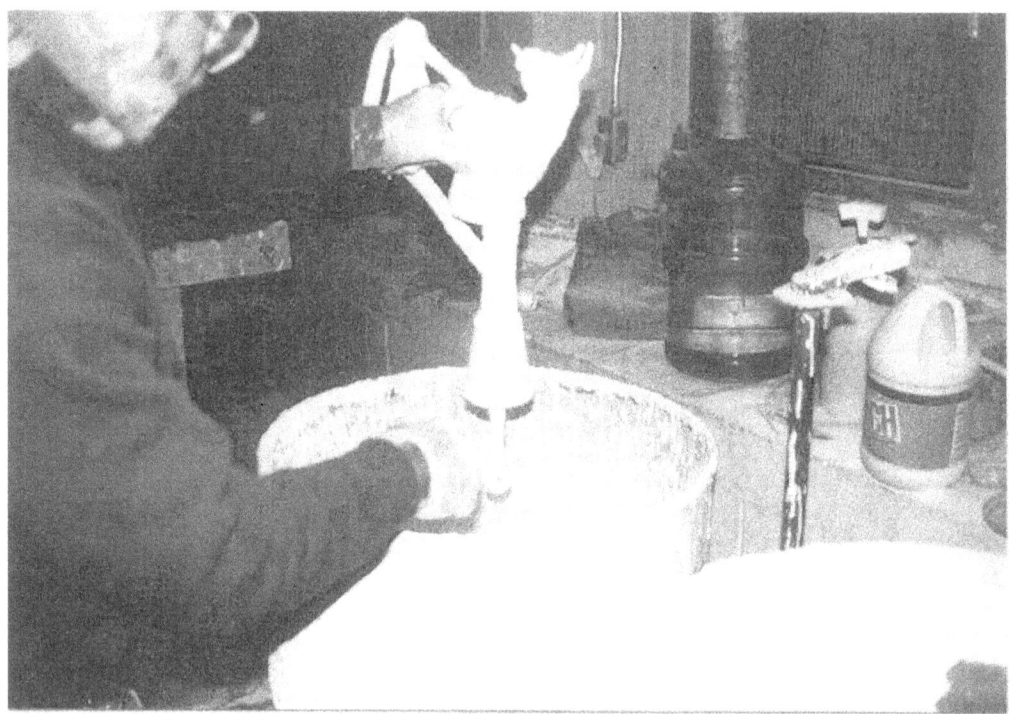

*Scott Art Castings closed when Dave Scott retired a few years ago.

Investing the Wax, continued

Step 2: Sand coating

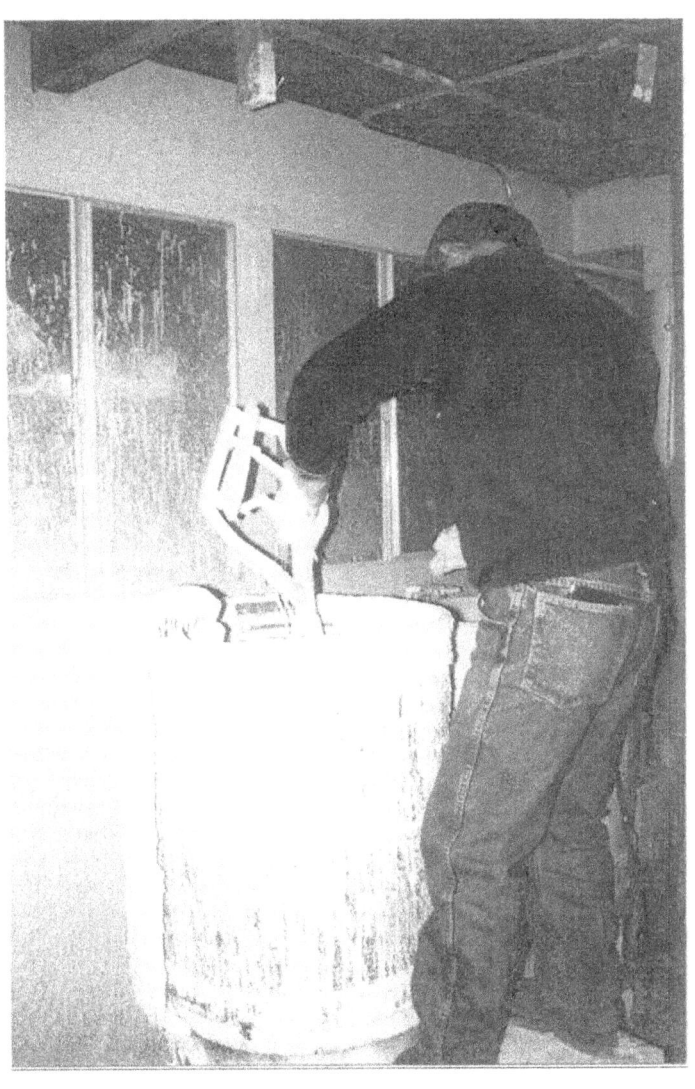

Once the wax has its first coat of ceramic slurry, it is then given a coating of very fine sand. The fine sand will pick up every detail on the surface of the piece, even fingerprints. An air hose under the barrel of sand blows through the sand at the press of a pedal to float the sand around the piece so there is no chance of pressure marring any detail.

Investing the Wax, continued

Multiple coats of ceramic slurry and sand are applied to the sculpture until the coating is thick enough to withstand the heat of bronze being poured into it.

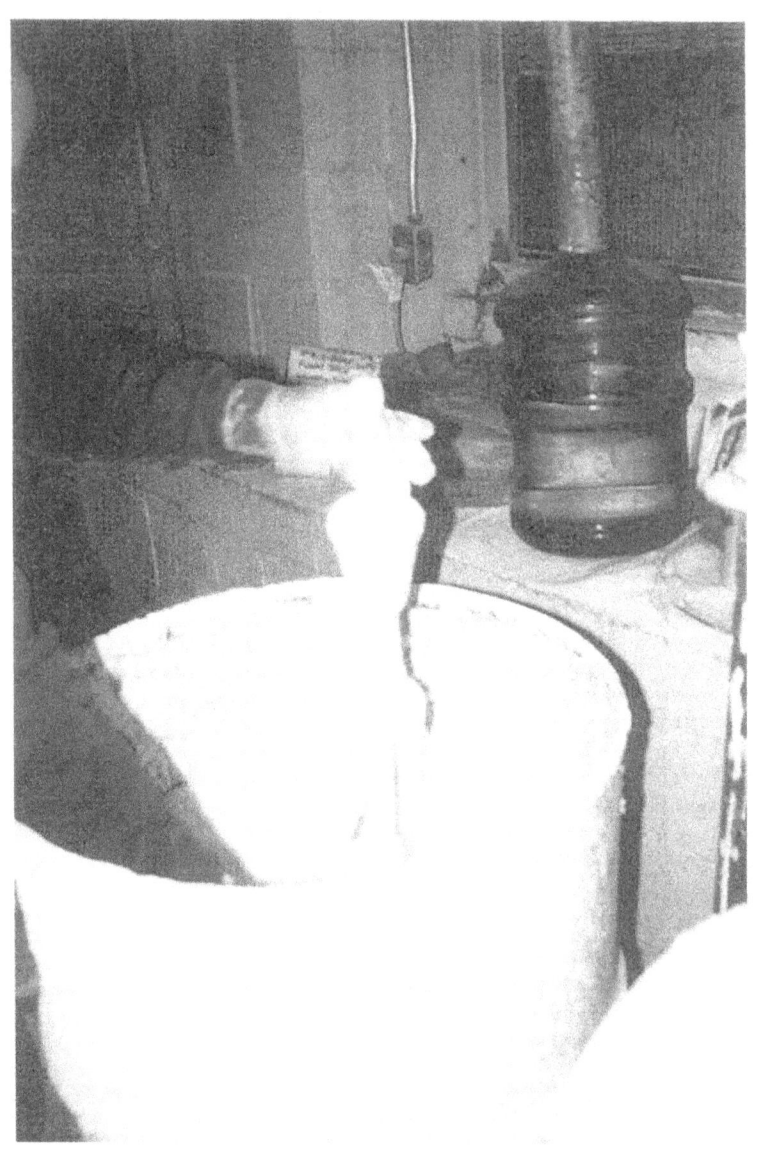

Drying the Investment

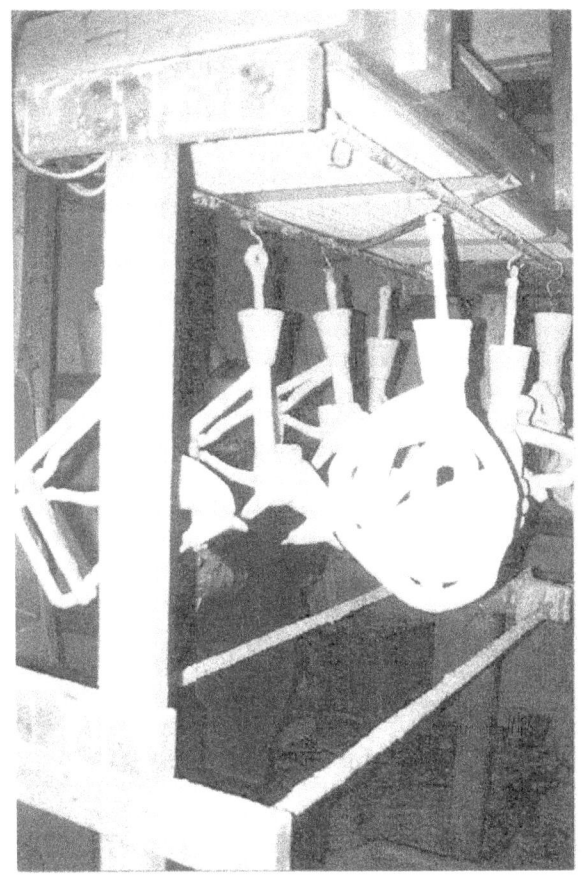

The invested waxes are hung to dry. This process takes about a week. You can see two front halves of "Presence" hanging on the far left of this rack. The pieces on the right hand rack are nearly dry, as is shown by their light color (which is orange, as opposed to the lime green of the wet pieces on the left).

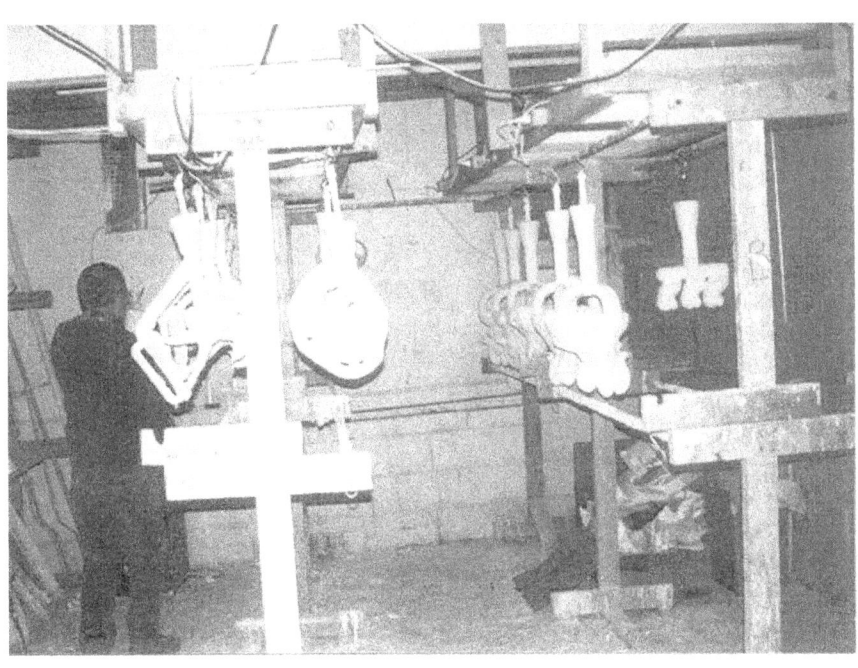

Burnout and Casting

The dried investment, also called the *shell*, is taken to a kiln where the wax is burned out (hence the "lost wax" description). Some foundries will also use an autoclave to make sure the ceramic shell mold is as clean as it can be. When the foundry is ready to cast the piece, they reheat the investment in a furnace near the *crucible* (the melting pot which holds the molten bronze). Hot bronze would crack a cold shell, so the investment must be hot before the liquid bronze can be poured into it. The shell is settled ina bed of sand, and the foundry workers pour the molten bronze from the crucible into the ceramic shell.

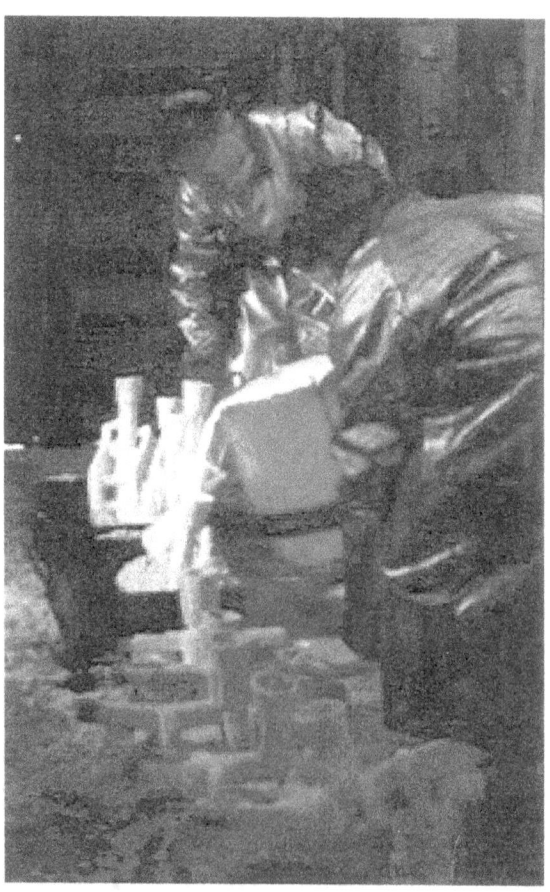

Shown: Scott employees pouring bronze into heated investments.

Blowouts

Each wax and each investment only get one chance to be a bronze. They can fail at any point in the process, which means the casters will have to start back at the beginning: pour a new wax, chase the wax, gate and sprue it, invest it, melt out the wax, reheat it, then try pouring bronze again.

If the shell cracks, it's called a "blowout" and is very dangerous to the crew, with 2000 to 2600 degree Fahrenheit molten bronze spewing from a crack or running across the floor. Blowouts are one reason the crew wears a lot of protecting clothing. Casting bronze is dangerous work.

Cleanup and Chasing the Bronze

Hammers are used to break the ceramic shell off the bronze (one wax, one shell [investment] per bronze sculpture, sometimes more than one if the piece had to be cast in sections). The remaining ceramic shell is sandblasted off the metal. The cleaned bronze is a light golden color.

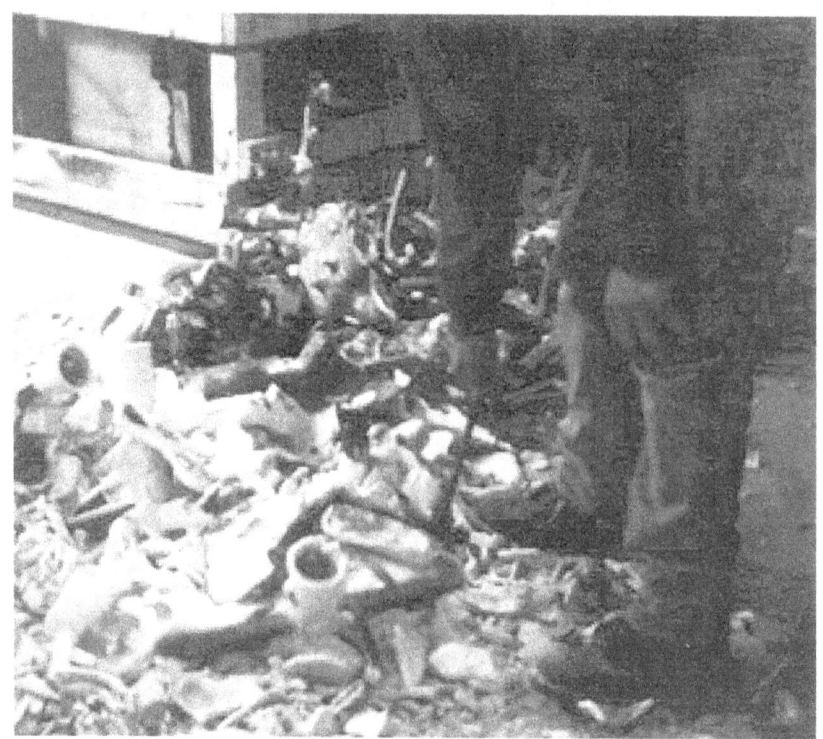

Shown: Scott employee using a hammer to break the investment off a freshly-cast bronze. He is standing by a pile of broken investment from other castings.

Chasing the Bronze

The bronze is taken to the finishing department. There, the piece will be "metal chased." The now-bronze sprues, gates and pour spout will be cut off and the nubs ground down to the sculpture's surface. Any pieces that were removed to cast separately will be welded into place. Weld marks will be ground down until they're smooth. Workers will insert rods or pins in legs or othe rsmall detail, if needed for support. The finishing department also replaces any texture the artist created on the original if it was damaged din the casting or chasing process.

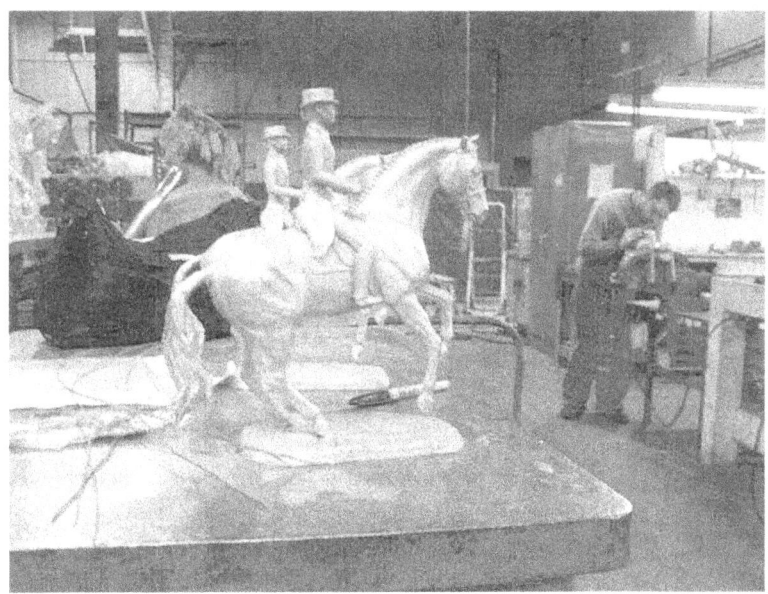

Shown: two "Harmony" castings at Tallix Foundry,* Beacon, New York, awaiting finishing.

*Tallix Foundry relocated and merged with Polich Foundry in Rock Tavern, New York. See Appendix 2 for contact information.

In Search of Perfection

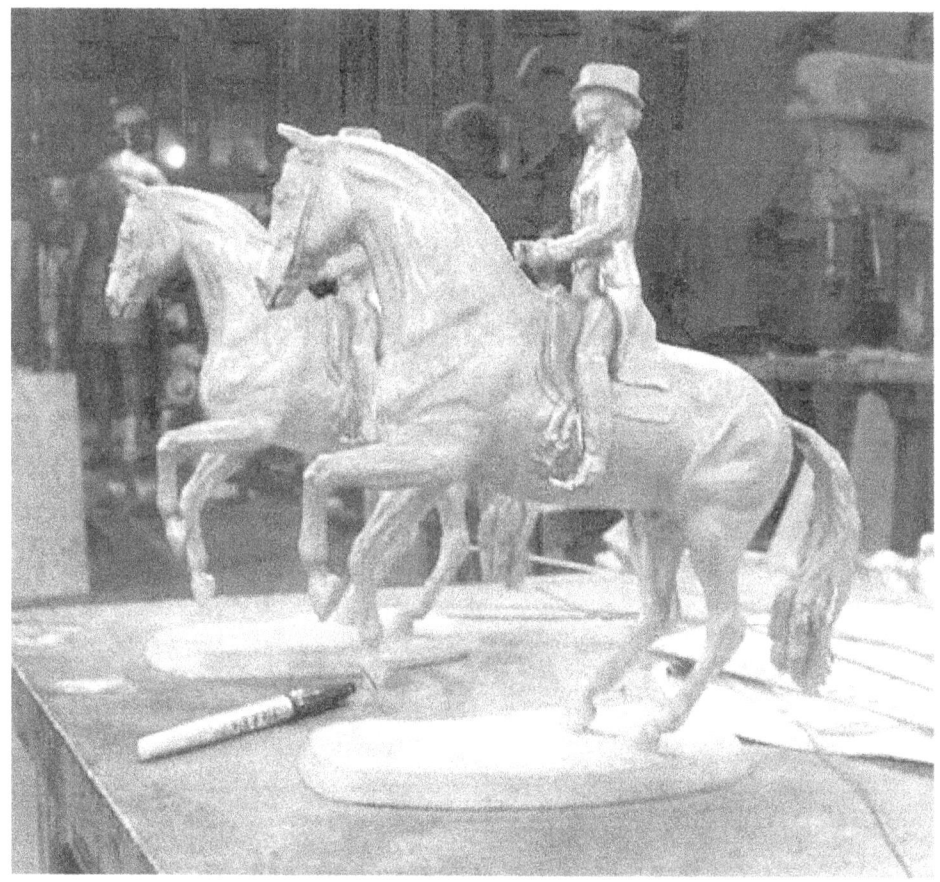

Two chased bronzes of "Harmony" waiting to be inspected. Note the felt-tipped pen and the marks on the horses hoof, the rider's boot, etc. I've marked places that need some repair work before finishing can be done.

Beginning of the End

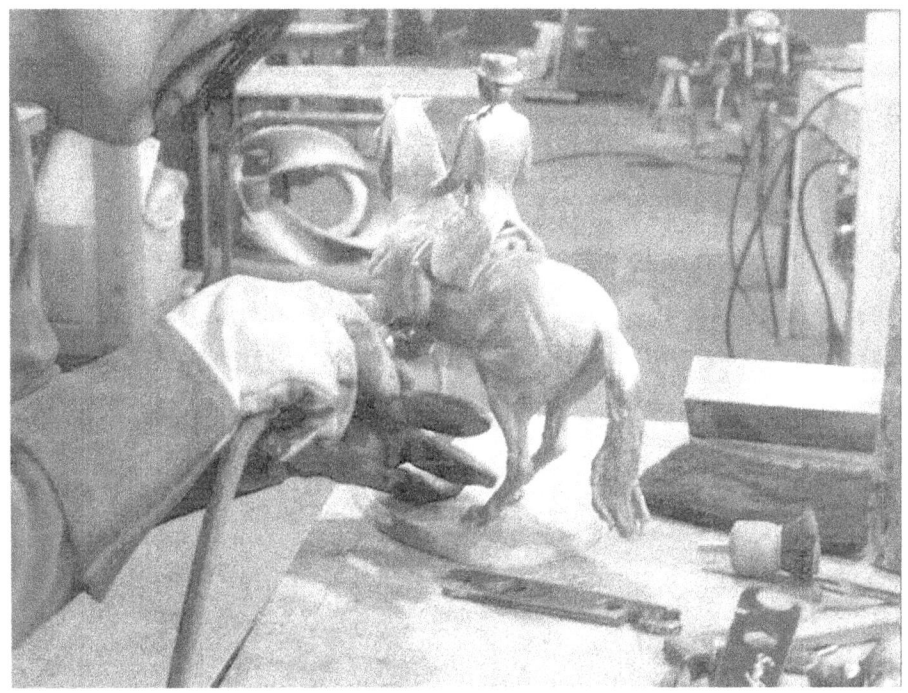

English stirrups, bits and reins are usually too small to be cast on pieces this size, so they are added by hand during the finishing phase. Here you see Insun Cafarelli, the head of Tallix's finishing department, grinding on a boot. The boot had to have metal added to it because the bronze didn't run correctly there, leaving a misshapen foot. After Insun worked on it, it was just as good as when I sculpted it.

Patination

The colors you see on bronze are called "patina." They are applied by a *patineur* (patina artist) in a process called "patination."

The metal is heated with a propane torch to open the pores of the metal before the patinas (various acids) are applied. When the metal cools, the color is locked into the pores of the metal. Many layers of patina are added to get the desired depth of color. The color is also affected by the temperature of the bronze when the color is applied.

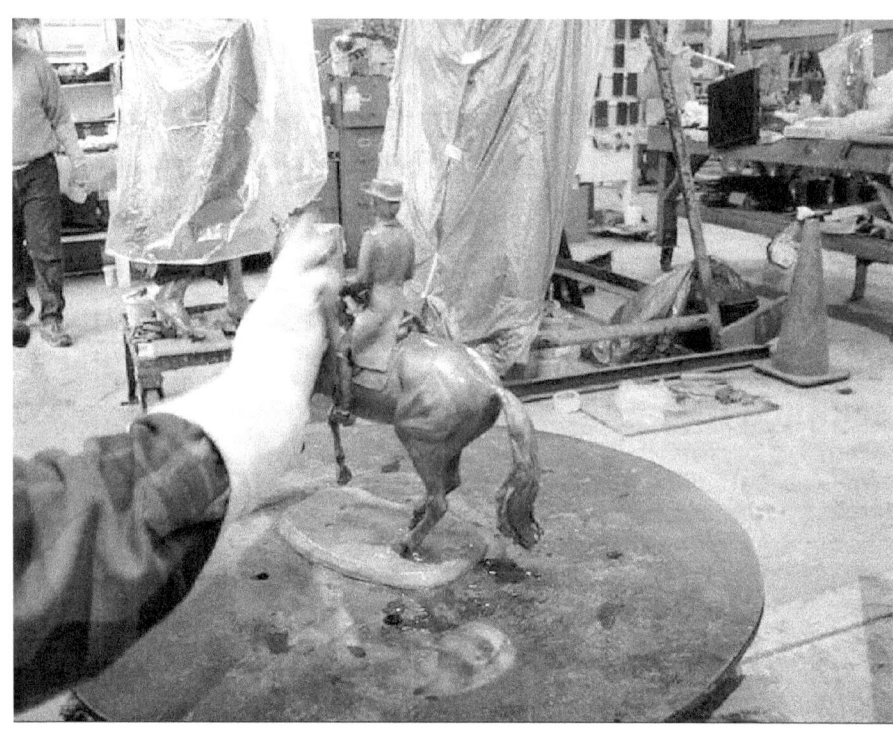

Continuing the Patina Work

Between layers of patina, the patineur rubs the bronze with a Scotch Brite^{TM} pad to buff the color off the high spots of the piece. By taking the color off the high spots, the bronze will look more dimensional, with the darkest color in the recesses, the medium color on the surface and the lightest color on the high spots (from being rubbed off).

I want translucent colors on my bronzes so the gleam of metal shows through the colors. Here the patineur is making each layer of color thin to achieve this effect.

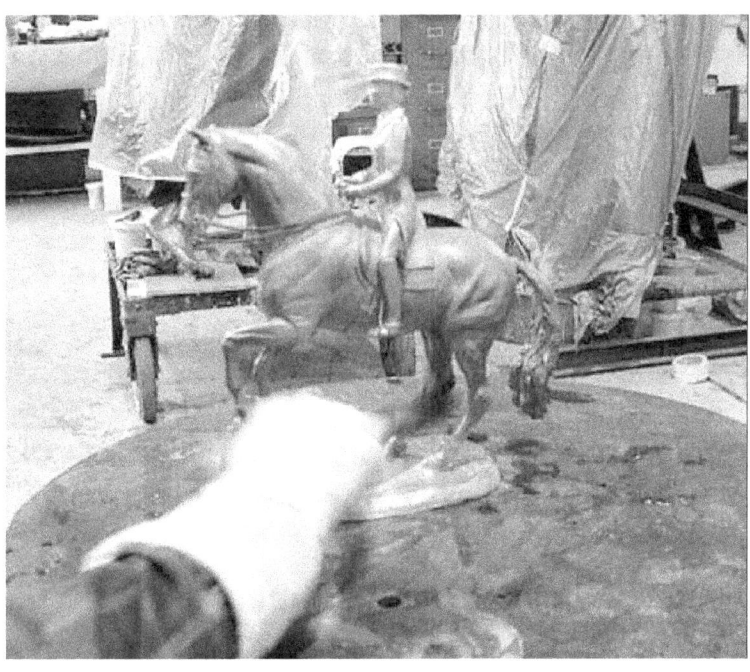

More Layers of Color

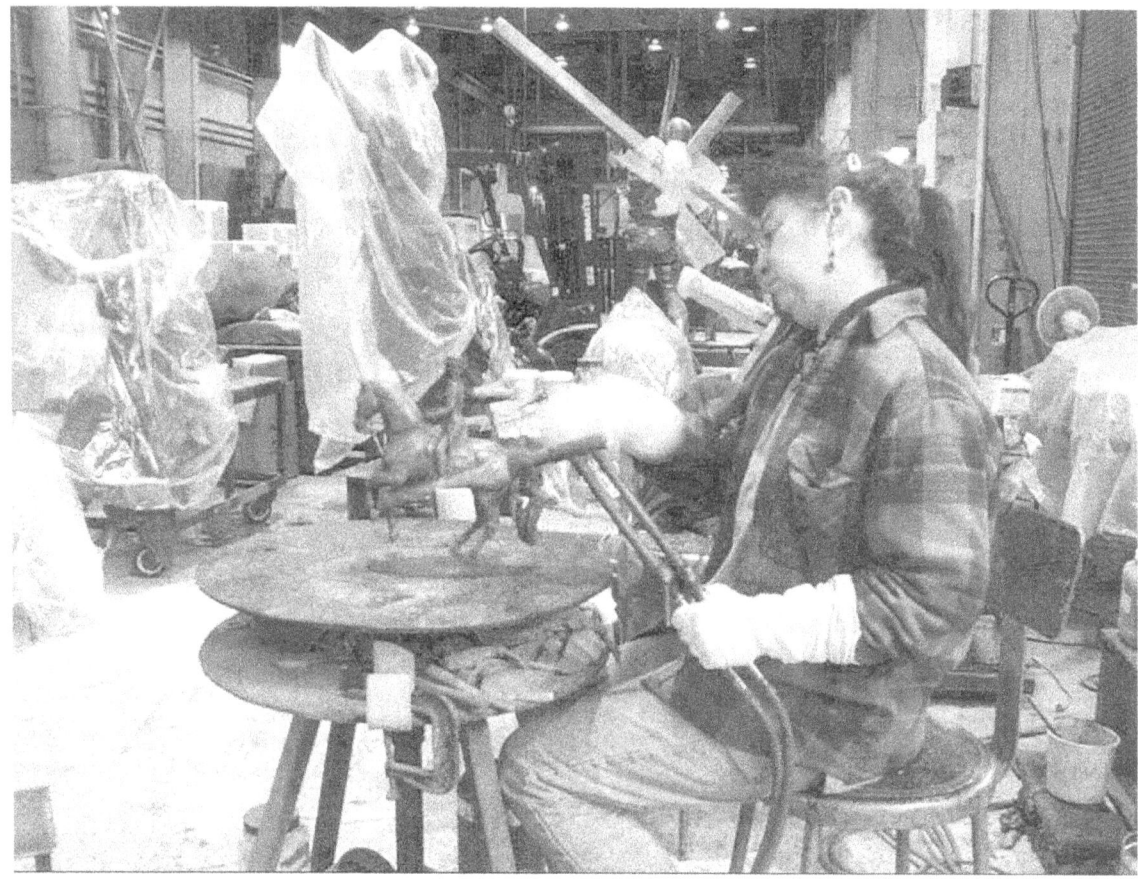

First heat is applied, then color (usually in the form of an acid), over and over, until the desired color is achieved.

Shown: Rosemary Rednour, head patineur at Tallix Foundry, Beacon, New York.

Nearly Done

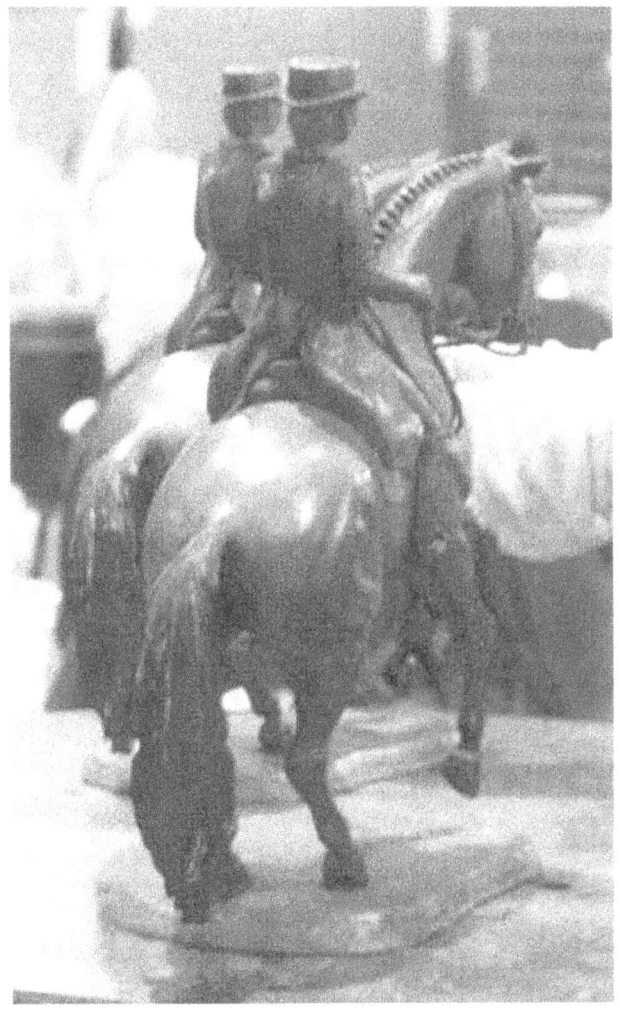

The coats, hats and boots on the riders, and the horses' manes, tails, lower legs, muzzles and eyes have a translucent layer of black patina applied for a more realistic effect.

A coating of paste wax is applied over the finished patina, then the sculpture is ready to mount on its base.

"Harmony"

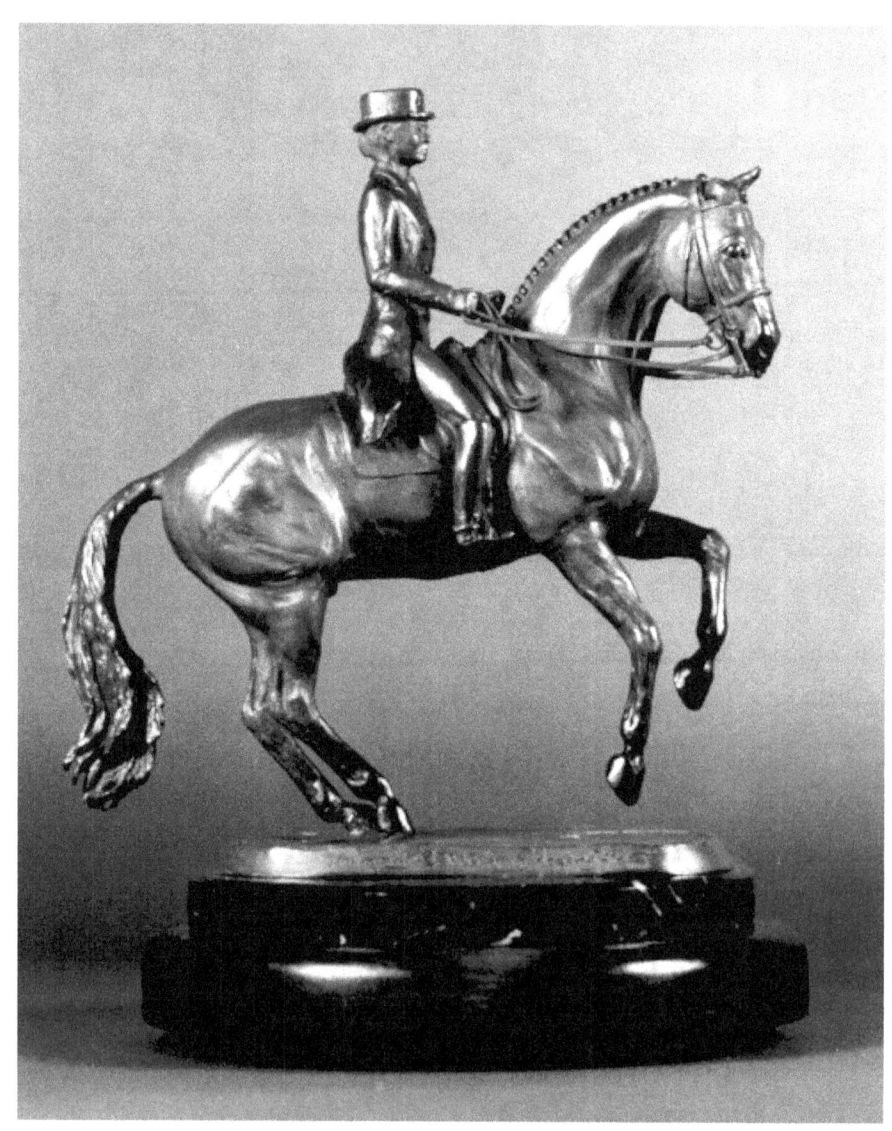

Appendix 4

The Bronze Pour—Two Methods

Tallix's Anti-Gravity Casting (TAG) was used for finely detailed pieces up to 40" x 40". TAG was called a "revolutionary vacuum process" created by Tallix Foundry, Beacon, New York (now merged with Polich Foundry as "PolichTallix" - see Appendix 2 for contact info). Tallix also did traditional open pour casting, sand casting and others, but the TAG system was unique to them at the time I was having "Harmony" cast there.

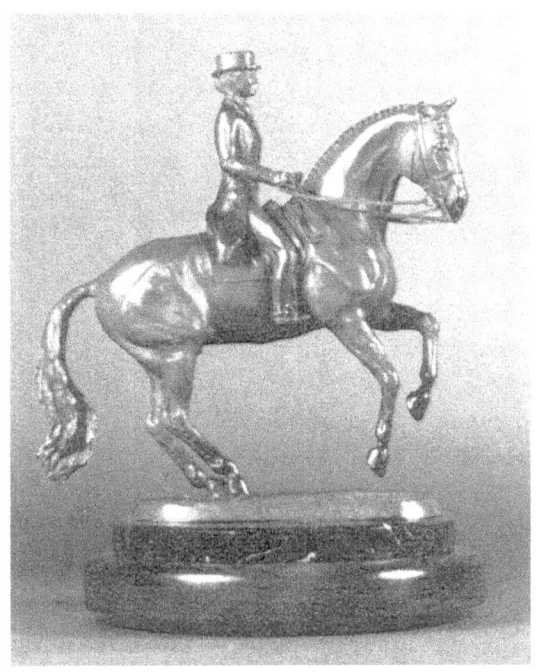

"Harmony," shown above, was cast with Tallix's TAG system.

The traditional "open pour" method of bronze casting is used at most foundries. The following pictures of an open pour are from Scott Art Casting, Indianapolis, Indiana (now closed due to the owner's retirement).

Below left: Tallix's furnace door is up, showing the interior where the investments have been heated to keep them from cracking when the hot bronze is poured.

Right: Scott Art Casting's furnaces are in the floor. The one on the right contains the molten bronze in a ceramic crucible which will be used for the pour.

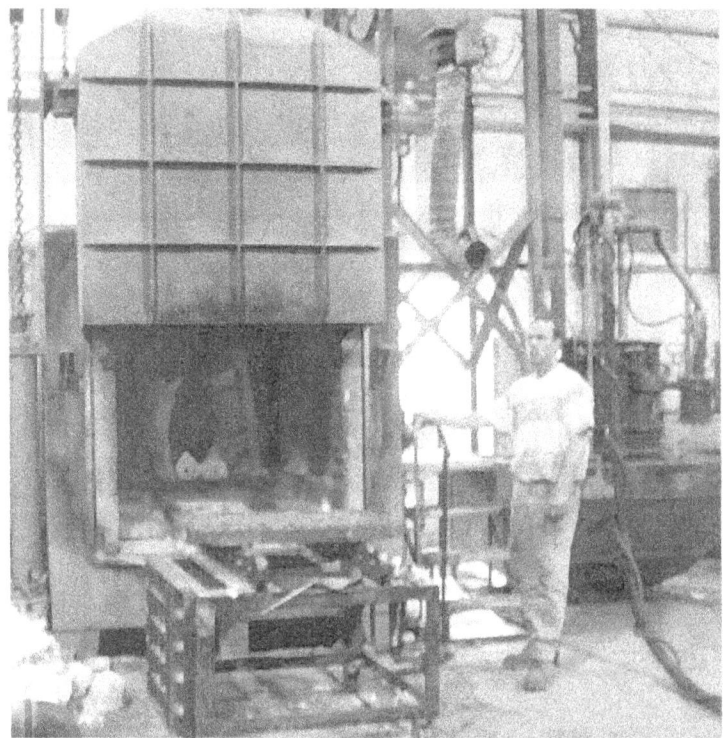

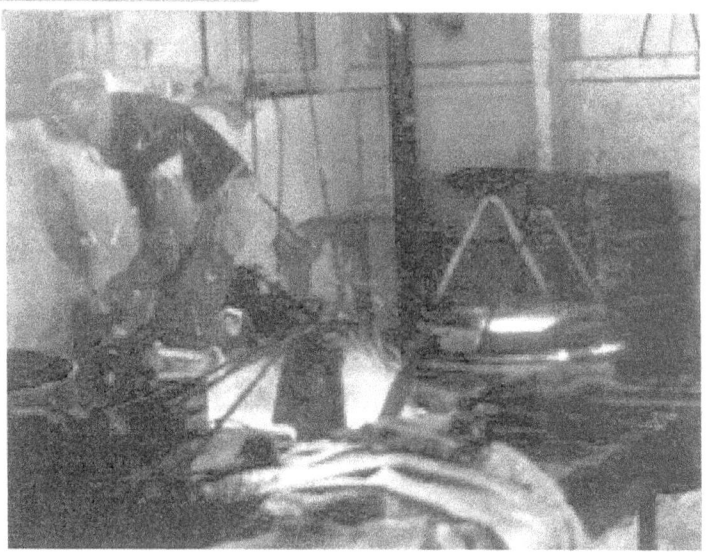

Setting Up the Investments

Tallix workers (left) have removed the top of the barrel where the bronze will be cast. One investment is put in the barrel, then surrounded by sand to secure it. The investment is mounted over a ceramic pipe which will draw the bronze up into the investment shell.

Scott workers (right) have their investments lined up in a pit with sand steadying them to be ready for the bronze pour.

The Scott employees each have an end of the bar that controls the crucible. The man on the right has two handles and he controls the pour. The man on the other end has only one handle and acts as a "pivot point" for the crucible.

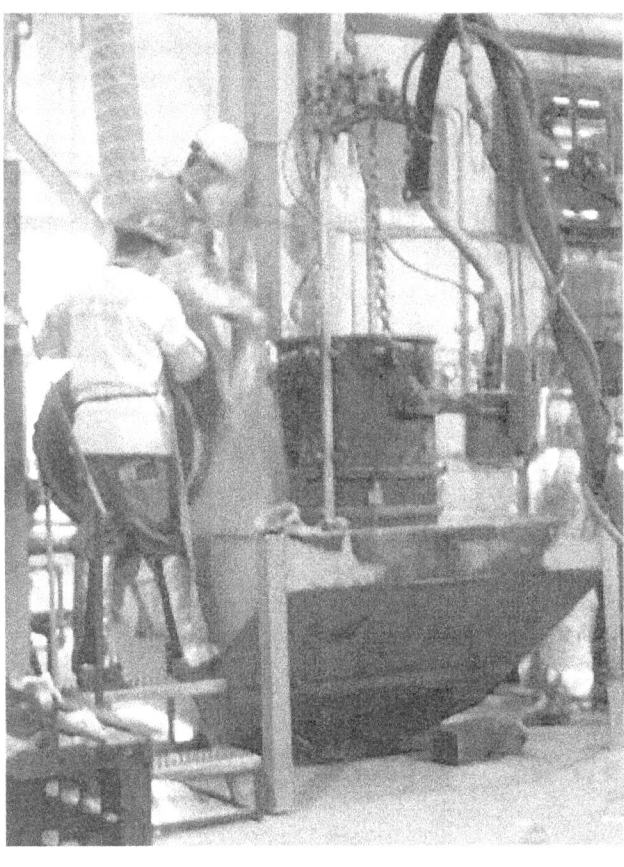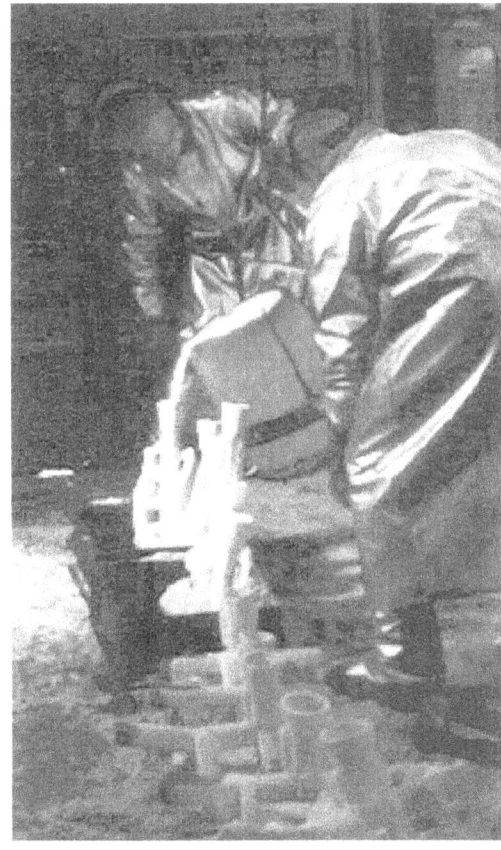

Checking the Temperature

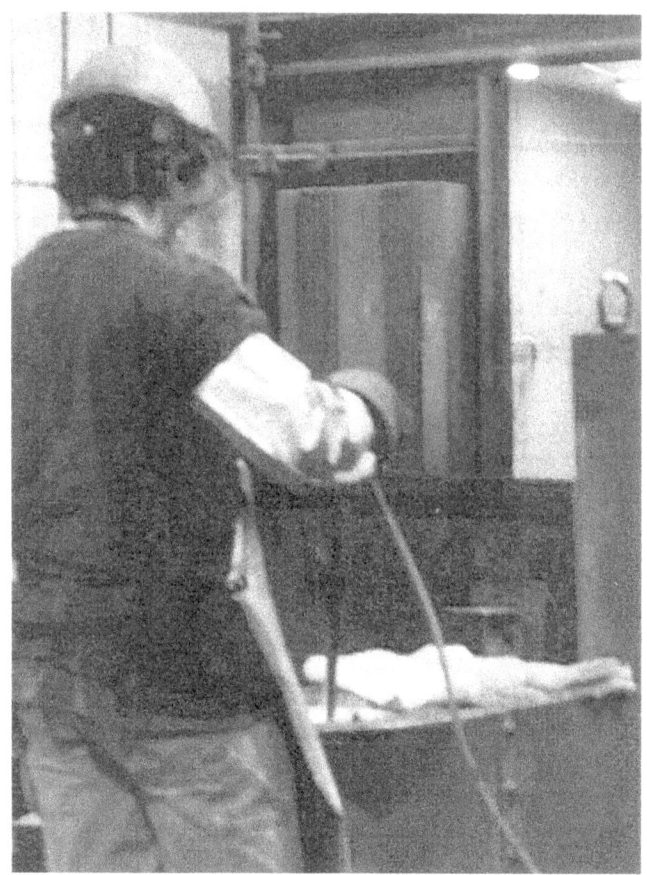

A Tallix worker checks the temperature of the molten bronze. Note this furnace is above ground level. The temperature necessary for this type of casting is 2600 degrees F., as opposed to 2200 degrees F. for an open pour.

Getting ready to cast

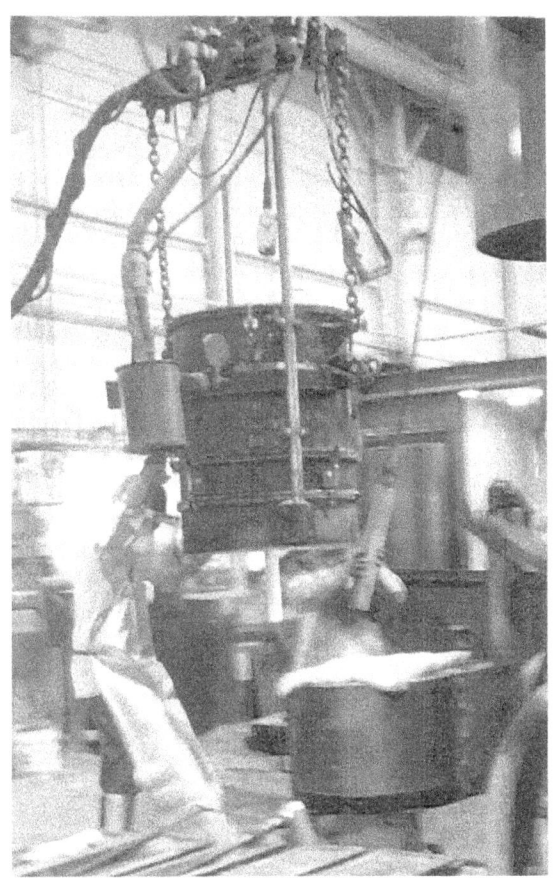

Tallix (left) uses a power winch to move the barrel with the snorkel (the pipe under the barrel) over the crucible.

Scott uses a manual winch to lift the crucible from the furnace.

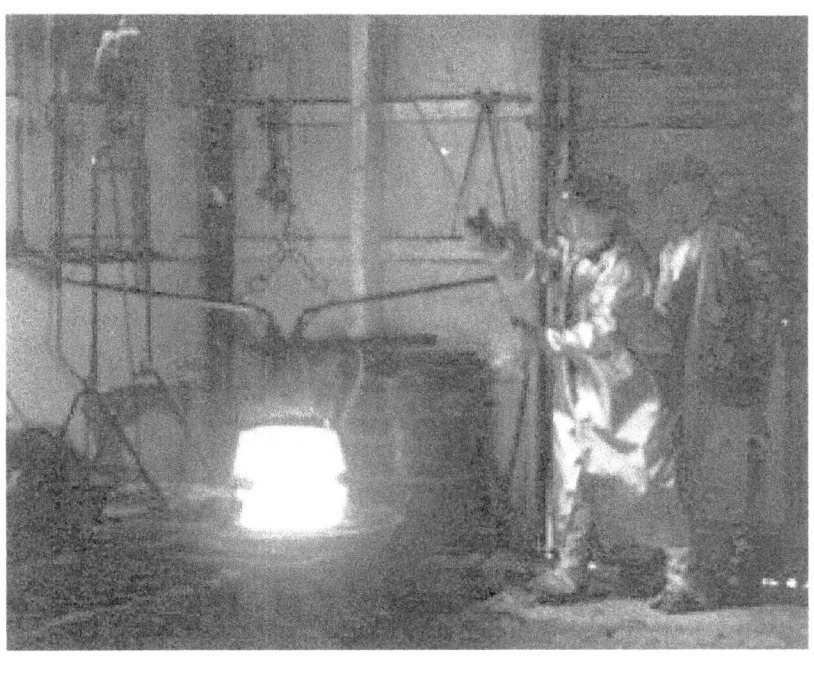

The Actual Pour

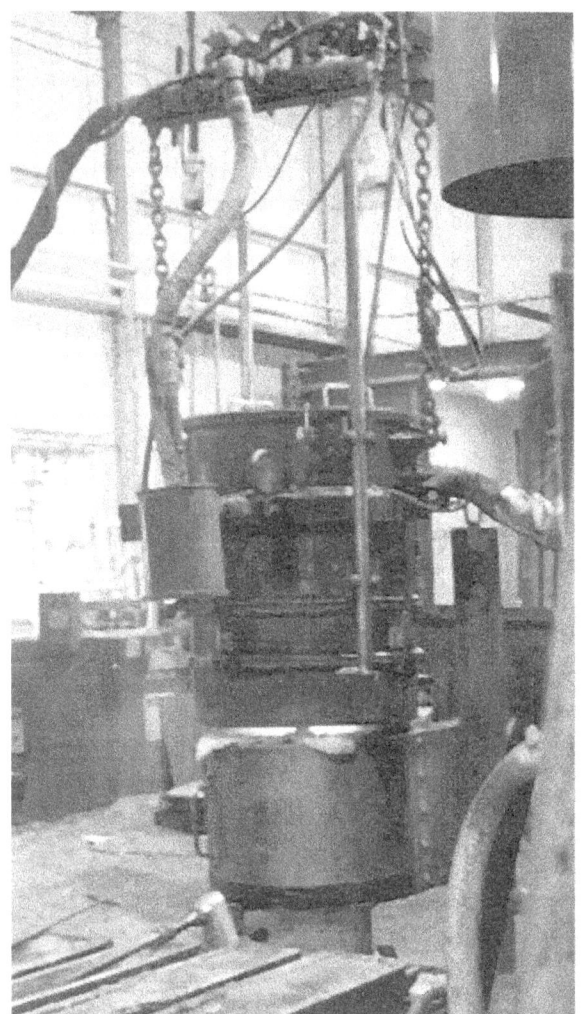

Tallix (left) lowers the barrel onto the furnace, and in seconds, the bronze goes up the tube and into the mold. Only one sculpture is cast at a time with this method.

Scott workers pour bronze into the investments, taking just a few seconds per sculpture. The process is amazingly fast in both cases

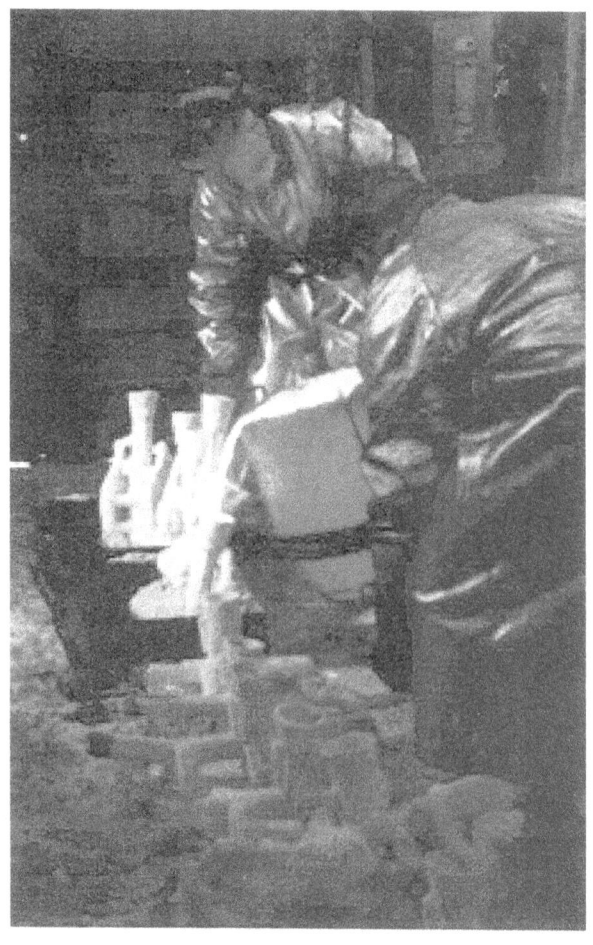

Plugging the Snorkel

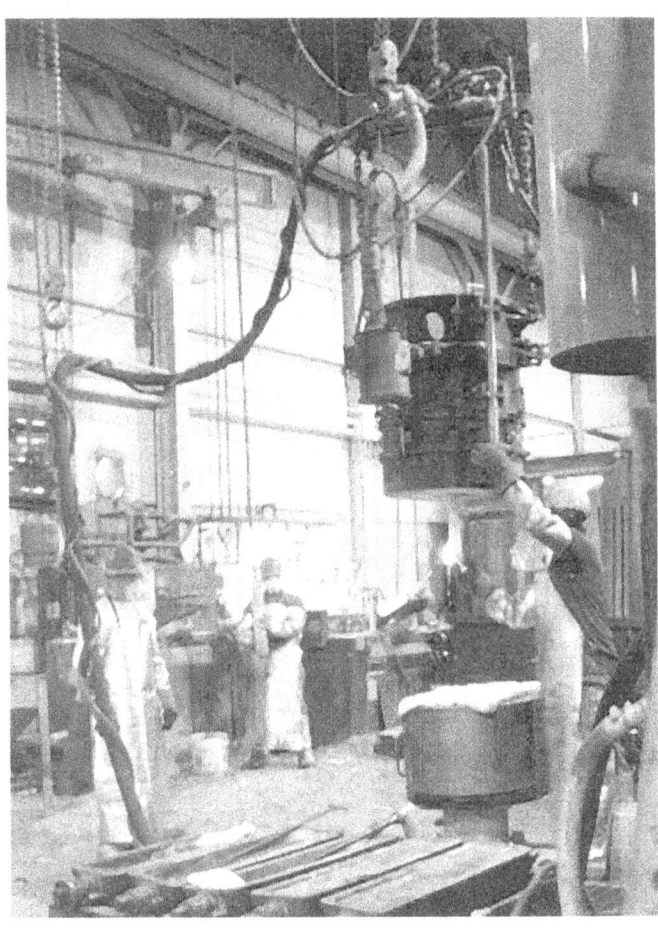

A Tallix worker has a plug in his gloved hand. Here he is plugging the snorkel so no bronze will pour out as the barrel goes back to its stand.

"Pigging"

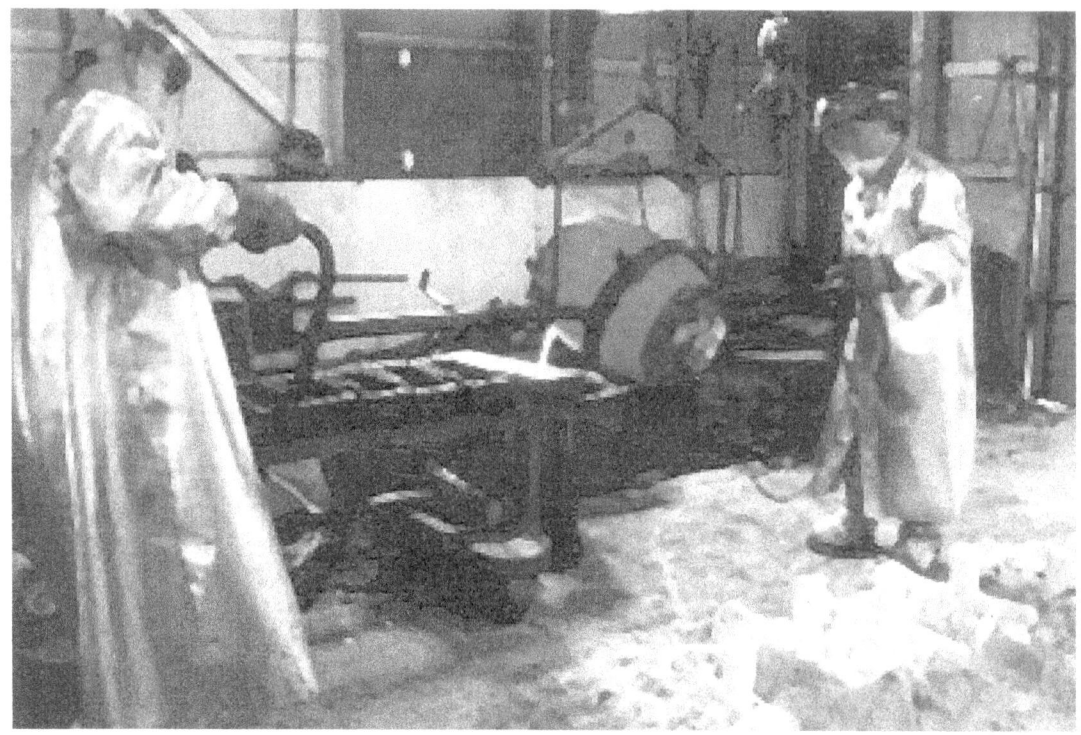

Scott workers pour leftover bronze into ingot molds, called "pigs." Large ingot molds are called "sows." These ingots are perfectly clean metal and can be reused for a future pour.

As It Cools . . .

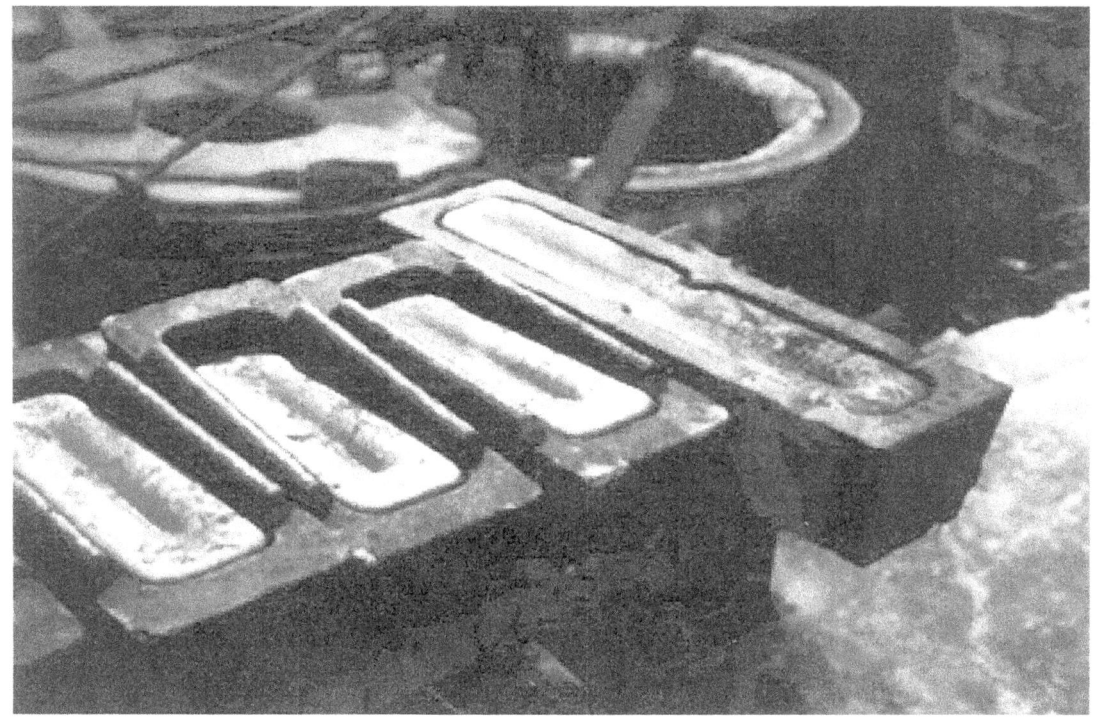

As bronze cools, it contracts. You can see where these ingots have pulled away from the sides of the molds and developed a line down the center. The bronze is still red-hot. This picture was taken moments after they were poured. (The large mold on the right is a "sow" and the rest are "pigs.")

Cooling Investment

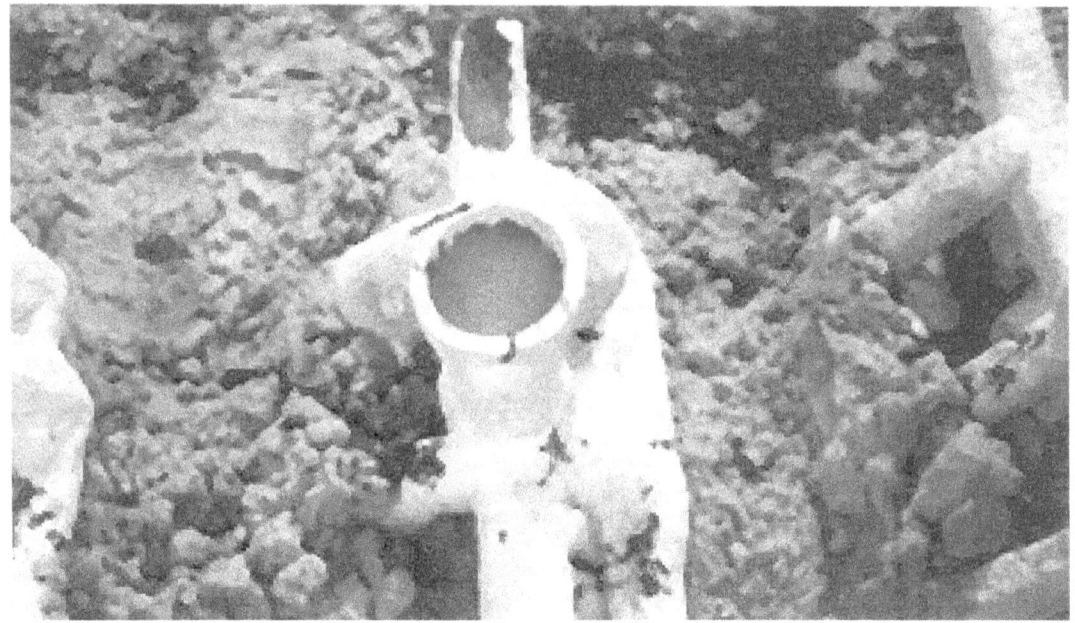

The bronze in this investment is cooling (although still red-hot) and a depression has formed in the metal as a result. The entire pour spout will be cut off and the bronze in it cleaned and reused, so this dip in the metal doesn't affect the sculpture itself.

Breaking off the Investment

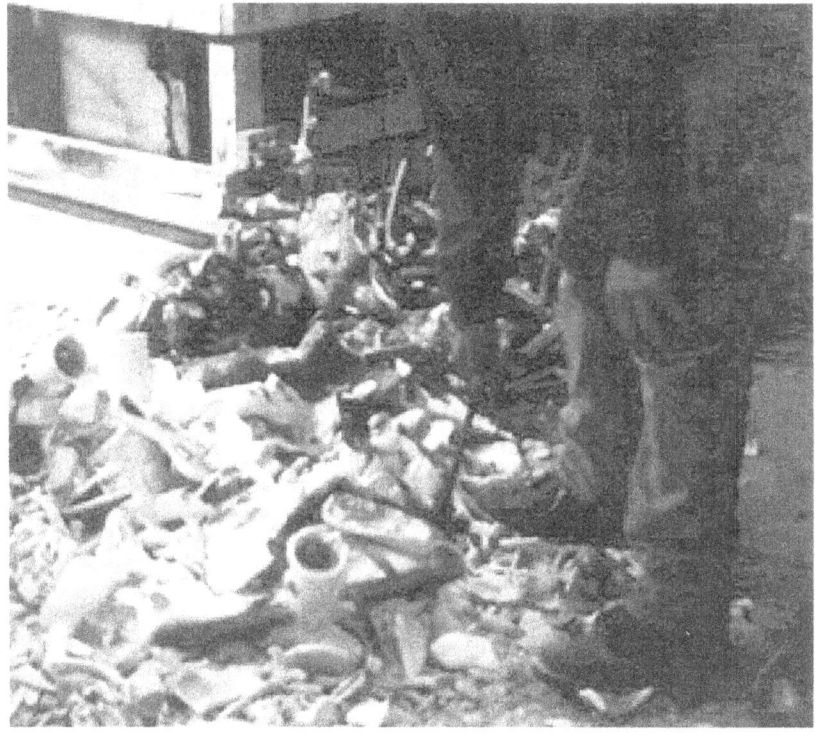

A Scott worker uses a hammer to break the investment off the still-warm sculptures. The investment is broken off as much as possible with the hammer. Then the sculpture will have the sprues and gating system cut off, leaving metal nubs on the sculpture. The sculpture will be sandblasted, then given to the finishing department to grind down the metal nubs, weld together any parts that were removed and restore any damaged detail (called "chasing the metal").

About the Author

A lifelong horsewoman born in Virginia, Lynda Sappington grew up riding hunters. Her husband's job took them to Ohio, where their children got into 4-H. Lynda taught them to ride, and both kids were champions in their show circuit in western and hunt seat events. Their daughter went on to eventing and then dressage, and is now an FEI level dressage rider and trainer. The variety of horses seen in these venues shows in Sappington's work, from backyard best friends to elite international-quality show horses.

Although primarily a self-taught sculptor, Sappington has honed her skills in workshops with Gwen Reardon, Kathleen Freidenberg, Anne Frey, Karen Kasper and Elin Pendleton of the American Academy of Equine Art, and Tuck Langland at the Scottsdale Artists School. Artists Shary Akers, Marcia Van Woert and C.R. Farmer were also generous in sharing art information and techniques, helping Lynda to grow greatly in her work when she was starting out.

Lynda's artwork has been featured in magazines such as *Dressage Today*, *The USDF Connection* and other publications, on the cover of *The Chronicle of the Horse* many times, and is in both private and corporate collections internationally.

Several of her bronze sculptures are trophies at prestigious shows – two of them, "Harmony" and "Presence," are the top two perpetual trophies at the Palm Beach Dressage Derby, Palm Beach, Florida. "Frolic" is a perpetual trophy for the US Dressage Federation, and "Friesian Elegance" is a world championship perpetual trophy for the Friesian Horse Association of North America (FHANA). The "Frolic" and "Elegance" trophies, as well as "Harmony" can all be seen at the Kentucky Horse Park, "Elegance" in the FHANA headquarters, "Frolic" and "Harmony" in the USDF headquarters, where "Harmony" is displayed in their Hall of Fame.

In January 2008, Lynda became a published novelist. *Star Sons – Dawn of the Two,* the first book in a fantasy series, is available on Amazon.com and many other outlets. The second *Star Sons* novel will be published in 2009. She also created, edited and wrote many articles for *ARTVoices,* an online magazine for and about artists that was online for three years, as well as contributing articles to various equine art publications.

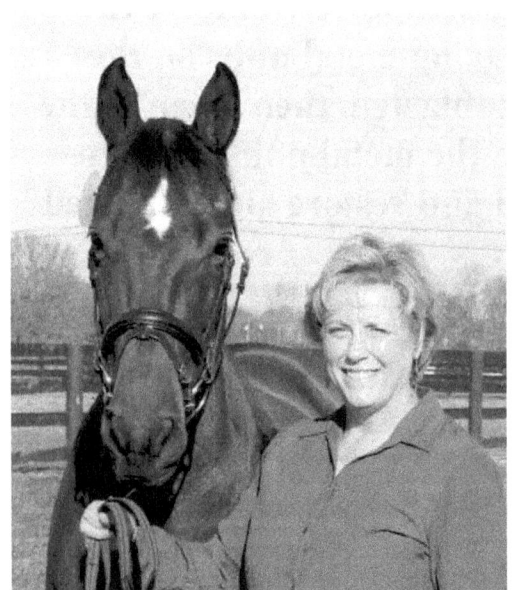

She is listed in Marquis' *Who's Who in America, Who's Who in American Women* and *Who's Who in the Midwest.*

Sappington and her husband, John, have owned and bred horses for over 35 years. After many years as a "horse show mother," Lynda bought a Quarter Horse gelding and showed him hunt seat and western for several years, winning many awards. In 2008, she decided to try dressage. Lynda is pictured at left with her new dressage horse, El Paso Aricos, who is certain to be the subject of future sculptures.

See Lynda's artwork and read samples of her writing at:

WWW.LYNDASAPPINGTON.COM

www.ingramcontent.com/pod-product-compliance
Lightning Source LLC
Chambersburg PA
CBHW080942170526
45158CB00008B/2352